Hugo's Simplified System

Greek
Phrase Book

Hugo's Language Books Limited

6th impression 1993

Compiled by
Lexus Ltd
with
Konstantinos Kontopidi-Greveniotis
and
Antigoni Kamberou Miller

*Facts and figures given in this book were
correct when printed. If you discover any
changes, please write to us.*

Set in 9/9 Times by Typesetters Ltd
and printed in England by
Page Bros, Norwich

CONTENTS

PREFACE

This is the latest in a long line of Hugo Phrase Books and is of excellent pedigree, having been compiled by experts to meet the general needs of tourists and business travellers. Arranged under the usual headings of 'Hotels', 'Motoring' and so forth, the ample selection of useful words and phrases is supported by an 1800-line mini-dictionary. By cross-reference to this, scores of additional phrases may be formed. There is also an extensive menu guide listing approximately 600 dishes or methods of cooking and presentation.

The pronunciation of words and phrases in the main text is imitated in English sound syllables, and highlighted sections illustrate some of the replies you may be given and the signs or instructions you may see or hear.

PRONUNCIATION

When reading the imitated pronunciation, stress that part which is underlined. Pronounce each syllable as if it formed part of an English word, and you will be understood sufficiently well. Remember the points below, and your pronunciation will be even closer to the correct Greek. Use our audio cassette of selected extracts from this book, and you should be word-perfect!

e: is always short, as in 'bed'.

i: is always long, as in 'Lolita'.

     (So when you see the imitation *ine,* remember to make this two syllables *ee-ne.* Similarly, *ne* and *me* should be kept short ... *don't* say 'nee' or 'mee'.)

h: is a guttural 'ch', as in the Scottish 'loch' (*don't* pronounce this as 'lock').

oo: long, as in 'moon'.

th: as in 'then' or 'the'. Notice this particularly, and *don't* confuse it with *TH* in small capitals.

TH as in 'theatre' or 'thin'.

g   should be a rolled guttural at the back of the throat.

Over the page is a futher guide to Greek pronunciation, alongside the Greek alphabet (in both capital and small letters).

THE GREEK ALPHABET

To help you read signs or notices printed in capital letters (which are sometimes quite unlike their small counterparts), we give below the Greek alphabet. Alongside each letter is its name, and a guide to its pronunciation. Until you get used to them, certain letters can be very confusing – for example, the *ro* which looks like an English P, or the lower case *ni* which closely resembles an English v (and is so similar to the small *ipsilon*).

letter		*name*	*pronunciation*
A	α	alfa	*a* as in 'father'.
B	β	vita	*v* as in 'victory'.
Γ	γ	ghamma	before *a, o* and *u* sounds, it is a guttural *gh* made at the back of the throat; before *e* and *i* sounds, it is like *y* in 'yes'.
Δ	δ	dhelta	*th* as in 'then'.
E	ε	epsilon	*e* as in 'end'.
Z	ζ	zita	*z* as in 'zest'.
H	η	ita	*i* as in 'Maria'.
Θ	θ	thita	*th* as in 'theatre'. (TH in the imitated pronunciation system.)
I	ι	yiota	before *a* and *o* sounds, like *y* in 'yes'; otherwise like *i* in 'Maria'.
K	κ	kapa	like *k* in 'king', but softer.
Λ	λ	lamdha	*l* as in 'love'.
M	μ	mi	*m* as in 'mother'.
N	ν	ni	*n* as in 'no'.

Ξ	ξ	ksi	*x* as in 'box', or *ks* as in 'books'.
Ο	ο	omikron	*o* as in 'orange'.
Π	π	pi	like *p* in 'Peter', but softer.
Ρ	ρ	ro	*r* as in 'Rome', trilled or rolled.
Σ	σ,ς	sighma	*s* as in 'sing'. The alternative small letter ς is used only at the end of a word.
Τ	τ	taf	like *t* in 'tea', but softer.
Υ	υ	ipsilon	*i* as in 'Maria'.
Φ	φ	fi	*f* as in 'friend'.
Χ	χ	hi	*ch* as in the Scottish 'loch'. But before *e* or *i* sounds like *h* in 'hue'.
Ψ	ψ	psi	like *ps* in 'lapse'.
Ω	ω	omegha	as *o* in 'orange'.

There are several different letter combinations which result in totally different sounds. For example, the word for 'England' which you put on your postcards from Greece is Αγγλία (or ΑΓΓΛΙΑ in capitals), and one word for 'waiter' is γκαρσόνι or γκαρσόη: the combination γκ produces a hard 'g' as in 'go', while γγ makes an 'ng' as in 'England'. Another combination that results in a new sound is ντ: this could be like the 'd' in 'dog', or it might begin with a slight 'n' sound ('nd' in 'bind'). One such example is the Greek for 'five', πέντε, which we imitate as *pede* in this book. Yet on the cassette (if you have bought the Travel Pack) you will hear the Greek speakers make it *pende*. Don't worry about this – use either, but keep the 'n' ineffectual! Of course, this particular example is plagued by its relationship to English words like ' pentagon' and all the others with a 'penta-' prefix, derived from the ancient Greek for 'five'. If you want to learn more about the modern language, buy our 'Greek in Three Months' book and cassettes!

7

USEFUL EVERYDAY PHRASES

Yes/No
Ναί/Όχι
ne/ohi

Thank you
Ευχαριστώ
efharisto

No thank you
Όχι, ευχαριστώ
ohi, efharisto

Please
Παρακαλώ
parakalo

I don't understand
Δεν καταλαβαίνω
then katalaveno

Do you speak English/French/German?
Μιλάτε Αγγλικά/Γαλλικά/Γερμανικά;
milate Aglika/Galika/Yermanika?

I can't speak Greek
Δεν μιλάω Ελληνικά
then milao Elinika

Please speak more slowly
Παρακαλώ, μιλάτε πιό αργά;
parakalo, milate pio arga?

Please write it down for me
Μου το γράφετε, παρακαλώ
moo to grafete, parakalo

Good morning/good afternoon/good night
Καλημέρα/καλησπέρα/καληνύχτα
kalimera/kalispera/kalinihta

Goodbye
Αντίο
adio

How are you?
Τι κάνεις;
ti kanis?

Excuse me please
Συγγνώμη, παρακαλώ
signomi, parakalo

Sorry!
Συγγνώμη!
signomi!

I'm really sorry
Ειλικρινά, λυπάμαι
ilikrina, lipame

Can you help me?
Μπορείς να με βοηθήσεις;
boris na me voiTHisis?

Can you tell me...?
Μου λέτε...;
moo lete...?

Can I have...?
Μπορώ να έχω...;
boro na eho...?

I would like...
Θα ήθελα...
THa iTHela...

Is there ... here?
Υπάρχει ... εδώ;
iparhi ... etho?

Where are the toilets?
Που είναι οι τουαλέτες;
poo ine i tooaletes?

Where can I get...?
Που μπορώ να πάρω...;
poo boro na paro...?

How much is it?
Πόσο κάνει;
poso kani?

Do you take credit cards?
Δέχεστε πιστωτικές κάρτες;
theheste pistotikes kartes?

Can I pay by cheque?
Μπορώ να πληρώσω με επιταγή;
boro na pliroso me epitayi?

What time is it?
Τι ώρα είναι;
ti ora ine?

I must go now
Πρέπει να πηγαίνω τώρα
prepi na piyeno tora

Cheers!
Εις υγείαν!
is iyian!

Go away!
Παράτα με!
paratame!

THINGS YOU'LL SEE OR HEAR

ανακοίνωση *anakinosi*	announcement
ΑΝΑΧΩΡΗΣΕΙΣ/αναχωρήσεις *anahorisis*	departures
ΑΝΟΙΚΤΑ/ανοικτά *anikta*	open
ΑΝΟΙΚΤΟΝ/ανοικτόν *anikton*	open
ΑΣΑΝΣΕΡ/ασανσέρ *asanser*	lift, elevator
αντίο *adio*	goodbye
απαγορεύεται το κάπνισμα *apagorevete to kapnisma*	no smoking
αργά *arga*	slow
αριστερά *aristera*	left
ΑΦΙΞΕΙΣ/αφίξεις *afixis*	arrivals
βιβλιοθήκη *vivlioTHiki*	library
ΓΥΝΑΙΚΩΝ/γυναικών *yinekon*	ladies
ΔΕΝ ΛΕΙΤΟΥΡΓΕΙ/δεν λειτουργεί *then litooryi*	out of order
δεξιά *thexia*	right
διάλειμμα *thialima*	interval
ΕΙΣΟΔΟΣ/είσοδος *isothos*	way in, entrance
έκθεση *ekTHesi*	exhibition, show room
έλεγχος *elenhos*	check, inspection

11

ελεύθερος *elefTHeros*	free
ΕΞΟΔΟΣ/έξοδος *exothos*	way out
ευχαριστώ *efharisto*	thank you
καλώς ήρθατε *kalos irTHate*	welcome
ΚΑΠΝΙΖΟΝΤΕΣ/καπνίζοντες *kapnizodes*	smokers
ΚΑΤΗΛΗΜΜΕΝΟΣ/κατηλημμένος *katilimenos*	engaged
ΚΙΝΔΥΝΟΣ/κίνδυνος *kinthinos*	danger
ΚΛΕΙΣΤΑ/κλειστά *klista*	closed
ΚΛΕΙΣΤΟΝ/κλειστόν *kliston*	closed
μέχρι *mehri*	until
μη *mi*	do not
ναί *ne*	yes
ορίστε; *oriste?*	can I help you?
όχι *ohi*	no
παρακαλώ *parakalo*	please, can I help you?
πεζοί *pezi*	pedestrians
προσοχή παρακαλώ *prosohi parakalo*	attention please
ΠΡΟΣΟΧΗ!/προσοχή! *prosohi*	caution!
ΣΥΡΑΤΕ/σύρατε *sirate*	pull
ΣΤΟΠ/στόπ *stop*	stop
στρίψατε *stripsate*	turn
ΣΧΟΛΕΙΟ/σχολείο *s-holio*	school
ΤΑΜΕΙΟ/ταμείο *tamio*	till, cash desk
ΤΕΛΩΝΕΙΟ/Τελωνείο *telonio*	Customs
ΤΟΥΡΙΣΤΙΚΗ ΑΣΤΥΝΟΜΙΑ/Τουριστική Αστυνομία *Tooristiki Astinomia*	Tourist Police
χαίρετε *herete*	hello
ωθήσατε *οTHisate*	push
ώρες λειτουργίας *ores litooryias*	opening hours

DAYS, MONTHS, SEASONS

Sunday	η Κυριακή	*i kiriaki*
Monday	η Δευτέρα	*i theftera*
Tuesday	η Τρίτη	*i triti*
Wednesday	η Τετάρτη	*i tetarti*
Thursday	η Πέμπτη	*i pembti*
Friday	η Παρασκευή	*i paraskevi*
Saturday	το Σάββατο	*to savato*

January	Ιανουάριος	*ianooarios*
February	Φεβρουάριος	*fevrooarios*
March	Μάρτιος	*martios*
April	Απρίλιος	*aprilios*
May	Μάιος	*maios*
June	Ιούνιος	*ioonios*
July	Ιούλιος	*ioolios*
August	Αύγουστος	*avgoostos*
September	Σεπτέμβριος	*septemvrios*
October	Οκτώβριος	*oktovrios*
November	Νοέμβριος	*noemvrios*
December	Δεκέμβριος	*thekemvrios*

Spring	η άνοιξη	*i anixi*
Summer	το καλοκαίρι	*to kalokeri*
Autumn	το φθινόπωρο	*to ftʜinoporo*
Winter	ο χειμώνας	*o himonas*
Christmas	τα Χριστούγεννα	*ta hristooyena*
Christmas Eve	η παραμονή Χριστουγέννων	*i paramoni hristooyenon*
Good Friday	η Μεγάλη Παρασκευή	*i megali paraskevi*
Easter	το Πάσχα	*to pas-ha*
New Year	η Πρωτοχρονιά	*i protohronia*
New Year's Eve	η παραμονή Πρωτοχρονιάς	*i paramoni protohronias*

13

NUMBERS

0	μηδέν *mithen*	5	πέντε *pede*
1	ένα *ena*	6	έξι *exi*
2	δύο *thio*	7	επτά *epta*
3	τρία *tria*	8	οχτώ *ohto*
4	τέσσερα *tesera*	9	εννιά *enia*

10	δέκα	*theka*
11	έντεκα	*edeka*
12	δώδεκα	*thotheka*
13	δεκατρία	*theka-tria*
14	δεκατέσσερα	*theka-tesera*
15	δεκαπέντε	*theka-pede*
16	δεκαέξι	*theka-exi*
17	δεκαεπτά	*theka-epta*
18	δεκαοχτώ	*theka-ohto*
19	δεκαεννιά	*theka-enia*
20	είκοσι	*ikosi*
21	εικοσιένα	*ikosi-ena*
22	εικοσιδύο	*ikosi-thio*
30	τριάντα	*triada*
31	τριανταένα	*triada-ena*
32	τριανταδύο	*triada-thio*
40	σαράντα	*sarada*
50	πενήντα	*penida*
60	εξήντα	*exida*
70	εβδομήντα	*evthomida*
80	ογδόντα	*ogthoda*
90	ενενήντα	*enenida*
100	εκατό	*ekato*
110	εκατόν δέκα	*ekaton theka*
200	διακόσια	*thiakosia*
1000	χίλια	*hilia*
1,000,000	ένα εκατομμύριο	*ena ekatomirio*

TIME

today	σήμερα	simera
yesterday	χτες	htes
tomorrow	αύριο	avrio
the day before yesterday	προχτές	prohtes
the day after tomorrow	μεθαύριο	meтнavrio
this week	αυτή την εβδομάδα	afti tin evthomatha
last week	την περασμένη εβδομάδα	tin perasmeni evthomatha
next week	την επομένη εβδομάδα	tin epomeni evthomatha
this morning	το πρωί	to proi
this afternoon	το απόγευμα	to apoyevma
this evening	το βράδυ	to vrathi
tonight	απόψε	apopse
yesterday afternoon	χτες τ'απόγευμα	htes t'apoyevma
last night	χτες τη νύχτα	htes ti nihta
tomorrow morning	αύριο το πρωί	avrio to proi
tomorrow night	αύριο το βράδυ	avrio to vrathi
in three days	σε τρεις μέρες	se tris meres
three days ago	πριν τρεις μέρες	prin tris meres
late	αργά	arga
early	νωρίς	noris
soon	σύντομα	sidoma
later on	αργότερα	argotera
at the moment	προς το παρόν	pros to paron
second	το δευτερόλεπτο	to thefterolepto
minute	το λεπτό	to lepto
ten minutes	δέκα λεπτά	theka lepta
quarter of an hour	ένα τέταρτο	ena tetarto

half an hour	μισή ώρα	misi ora
three quarters of an hour	τρία τέταρτα της ώρας	tria tetarta tis oras
hour	η ώρα	i ora
day	η μέρα	i mera
week	η εβδομάδα	i evthomatha
fortnight, 2 weeks	σε δύο εβδομάδες	se thio evthomathes
month	ο μήνας	o minas
year	ο χρόνος	o hronos

TELLING THE TIME

In Greek you always put the hour first and then use the word 'ke' (και) to denote the minutes 'past' the hour and 'para' (παρά) for the minutes 'to' the hour (e.g. 5.20 = '5 ke 20'; 5.40 = '6 para 20'). The 24-hour clock is used officially in timetables and enquiry offices. Don't forget that Greek Standard Time is always two hours ahead of Greenwich Mean Time.

one o'clock	μία η ώρα	mia i ora
ten past one	μία και δέκα	mia ke theka
quarter past one	μία και τέταρτο	mia ke tetarto
twenty past one	μία και είκοσι	mia ke ikosi
half past one	μία και μισή	mia ke misi
twenty to two	δύο παρά είκοσι	thio para ikosi
quarter to two	δύο παρά τέταρτο	thio para tetarto
ten to two	δύο παρά δέκα	thio para theka
two o'clock	δύο η ώρα	thio i ora
13.00 (1 pm)	δεκατρείς	theka-tris
16.30 (4.30 pm)	δεκαέξι και τριάντα	theka-exi ke triada
20.10 (8.10 pm)	είκοσι και δέκα	ikosi ke theka
at half past five	στις πέντε και μισή	stis pede ke misi
at seven o'clock	στις επτά	stis efta
noon	το μεσημέρι	to mesimeri
midnight	τα μεσάνυχτα	ta mesanihta

HOTELS

Depending on the visitor's preferences and on what he is prepared to spend, there is a wide choice of hotels, service flats, self-catering accommodation and rooms in private houses.

Hotels are divided into six categories; De Luxe or AA, 1st to 5th Class or A to E. In most hotels a 15% service charge is added to your bill. The Greek National Tourist Organisation (G.N.T.O.) publishes useful information with an up-to-date list of addresses and the facilities available. If you are travelling in the high season it is always advisable to book accommodation in advance in the more popular areas.

USEFUL WORDS AND PHRASES

balcony	το μπαλκόνι	*to balkoni*
bathroom	το λουτρό	*to lootro*
bed	το κρεβάτι	*to krevati*
bedroom	το υπνοδωμάτιο	*to ipnothomatio*
bill	ο λογαριασμός	*o logariasmos*
breakfast	το πρωινό	*to proino*
dining room	η τραπεζαρία	*i trapezaria*
dinner	το δείπνο	*to thipno*
double room	το διπλό δωμάτιο	*to thiplo thomatio*
foyer	το φουαγιέ	*to fooaye*
full board	η φουλ-πανσιόν	*i fool-pansion*
half board	η ντεμί-πανσιόν	*i demi-pansion*
hotel	το ξενοδοχείο	*to xenothohio*
key	το κλειδί	*to klithi*
lift, elevator	το ασανσέρ	*to asanser*
lounge	το σαλόνι	*to saloni*
lunch	το γεύμα	*to yevma*
manager	ο διευθυντής	*o thi-efthidis*
receipt	η απόδειξη	*i apothixi*

HOTELS

reception	η ρεσεψιόν	*i resepsion*
receptionist	ο ρεσεψιονίστας	*o resepsionistas*
restaurant	το εστιατόριο	*to estiatorio*
room	το δωμάτιο	*to thomatio*
room service	το σέρβις δωματίου	*to servis thomatioo*
shower	το ντους	*to doos*
single room	το μονό δωμάτιο	*to mono thomatio*
toilet	η τουαλέτα	*i tooaleta*
twin room	το δωμάτιο με δύο κρεβάτια	*to thomatio me thio krevatia*

Have you any vacancies?
Εχετε κενά δωμάτια;
ehete kena thomatia?

I have a reservation
Εχω κλείσει δωμάτιο
eho klisi thomatio

I'd like a single room
Θα ήθελα ένα μονό δωμάτιο
THa iTHela ena mono thomatio

I'd like a double room
Θα ήθελα ένα δωμάτιο με διπλό κρεβάτι
THa iTHela ena thomatio me thiplo krevati

I'd like a twin room
Θα ήθελα ένα δωμάτιο με δύο κρεβάτια
THa iTHela ena thomatio me thio krevatia

I'd like a room with a bathroom/balcony
Θα ήθελα ένα δωμάτιο με μπάνιο/μπαλκόνι
THa iTHela ena thomatio me banio/balkoni

I'd like a room for one night/three nights
Θα ήθελα ένα δωμάτιο γιά μία νύχτα/τρεις νύχτες
THa iTHela ena thomatio ya mia nihta/tris nihtes

What is the charge per night?
Πόσο στοιχίζει η διανυκτέρευση;
poso stihizi i thianikterefsi?

REPLIES YOU MAY BE GIVEN

Then iparhoon mona/thipla thomatia kena
There are no single/double rooms left

Imaste yemati
We're full

Parakalo, plironete prokatavolika?
Please pay in advance

Parakalo, afinete to thiavatirio sas etho?
Please leave your passport here

I don't know yet how long I'll stay
Δεν ξέρω ακόμα πόσο καιρό θα μείνω
then xero akoma poso kero THa mino

When is breakfast/dinner?
Πότε έχει πρωινό/δείπνο;
pote ehi proino/thipno?

Would you have my luggage brought up?
Θα μου φέρετε τις βαλίτσες μου;
THa moo ferete tis valitses moo?

19

Please call me at ... o'clock
Παρακαλώ ειδοποιήστε με στις...
parakalo ithopi-isteme stis...

Can I have breakfast in my room?
Μπορώ να πάρω το πρωινό στο δωμάτιό μου;
boro na paro to proino sto thomatio moo?

I'll be back at ... o'clock
Θα επιστρέψω στις...
THA epistrepso stis...

My room number is...
Ο αριθμός του δωματίου μου είναι...
o ariTHmos too thomatioo moo ine...

I'm leaving tomorrow
Φεύγω αύριο
fevgo avrio

Can I have the bill please?
Τον λογαριασμό παρακαλώ
ton logariasmo parakalo

Can you get me a taxi?
Μου καλείτε ένα ταξί;
moo kalite ena taxi?

Can you recommend another hotel?
Μπορείτε να μου προτείνετε κάποιο άλλο ξενοδοχείο;
borite na moo protinete kapio alo xenothohio?

THINGS YOU'LL SEE OR HEAR

ασανσέρ	*asanser*	lift, elevator
γκαράς	*garaz*	garage
δείπνο	*thipno*	dinner
διπλό δωμάτιο	*thiplo thomatio*	double room
δωμάτια	*thomatia*	rooms
είσοδος	*isothos*	entrance
ενοικιάζονται δωμάτια	*enikiazode thomatia*	rooms to let
ΕΟΤ		Greek Tourist Organisation
έξοδος κινδύνου	*exothos kinthinoo*	emergency exit
εστιατόριο	*estiatorio*	restaurant
ισόγειο	*isoyio*	ground floor
λογαριασμός	*logariasmos*	bill
λουτρό	*lootro*	bathroom
μονό δωμάτιο	*mono thomatio*	single room
ντους	*doos*	shower
ξενοδοχείο	*xenothohio*	hotel
πλήρες	*plires*	full, no vacancies
πρωινό	*proino*	breakfast
πρώτος όροφος	*protos orofos*	first floor
ρεσεψιόν	*resepsion*	reception
σκάλες	*skales*	stairs
σύρατε	*sirate*	pull
τουαλέτες	*tooaletes*	toilets
υπόγειο	*ipoyio*	basement
φαγητό	*fayito*	meal, lunch
ωθήσατε	*oTHisate*	push

CAMPING & CARAVANNING

There are plenty of organised camping sites run by the Greek National Tourist Organisation and often these are situated in some of the most picturesque parts of the country. Campsites are usually open from March to November. In addition to the state-run campsites there are also a large number run by private individuals under licence. Further details about these camping sites can be supplied by G.N.T.O. information offices as well as by the Greek Tourist Police, who will have an office in every major town. If you are camping in Greece you should remember that it is forbidden to camp anywhere other than in a proper site.

Youth hostels are open to members of the YHA with stays being limited to ten nights.

USEFUL WORDS AND PHRASES

bucket	ο κουβάς	o koovas
campfire	φωτιά	fotia
to go camping	κατασκηνώνω	kataskinono
campsite	το κάμπινγκ	to 'camping'
caravan (R.V.)	το τροχόσπιτο	to trohospito
caravan site	το κάμπινγκ γιά τροχόσπιτα	to 'camping' ya trohospita
cooking utensils	τα σκεύη μαγειρικής	ta skevi mayirikis
drinking water	το πόσιμο νερό	to posimo nero
ground sheet	ο μουσαμάς	o moosamas
to hitch-hike	κάνω ωτο-στόπ	kano oto-stop
rope	το σχοινί	to s-hini
rubbish	τα σκουπίδια	ta skoopithia
rucksack	το σακίδιο	to sakithio
saucepans	τα κατσαρολικά	ta katsarolika
sleeping bag	το σλίπινιγκ μπαγκ	to 'sleeping bag'
tent	η σκηνή	i skini
youth hostel	ο ξενώνας νέων	o xenonas neon

Can I camp here?
Μπορώ να κατασκηνώσω εδώ;
boro na kataskinoso etho?

Can we park the caravan (trailer) here?
Μπορούμε να παρκάρουμε το τροχόσπιτο εδώ;
boroome na parkaroome to trohospito etho?

Where is the nearest campsite?
Που είναι το πλησιέστερο κάμπινγκ;
poo ine to plisi-estero 'camping'?

What is the charge per night?
Πόσο στοιχίζει η διανυκτέρευση;
poso stihizi i thianikterefsi?

What facilities are there?
Τι ευκολίες υπάρχουν εκεί;
ti efkoli-es iparhoon eki?

Can I light a fire here?
Μπορώ ν' ανάψω φωτιά εδώ;
boro n' anapso fotia etho?

Where can I get...?
Που μπορώ να βρω...;
poo boro na vro...?

Is there drinking water here?
Υπάρχει πόσιμο νερό εδώ;
iparhi posimo nero etho?

THINGS YOU'LL SEE OR HEAR

απαγορεύεται το κάμπινγκ *apagorevete to 'camping'*	no camping
κάμπινγκ *'camping'*	campsite
κουβέρτα *kooverta*	blanket
κουζίνα *koozina*	kitchen
νερό *nero*	water
ντους *doos*	shower
ξενώνας νέων *xenonas neon*	youth hostel
πόσιμο νερό *posimo nero*	drinking water
ριμουλκό *rimoolko*	trailer (camping etc)
σκηνή *skini*	tent
σλίπινγκ μπαγκ *'sleeping bag'*	sleeping bag
ταυτότητα *taftotita*	pass, identity card
τιμή *timi*	charges
τουαλέτες *tooaletes*	toilets
τροχόσπιτα *trohospita*	caravans, trailers (R.V.)
φως *fos*	light
φωτιά *fotia*	fire
χρησιμοποιείται... *hrisimopi-ite...*	use...

MOTORING

Most roads in Greece are single-lane only. The national highways (*eTHniki*) are the best to use, as they often have crawler lanes for heavy vehicles, which makes overtaking much easier. If you drive to Greece via Austria and Yugoslavia, entering the country near Thessaloniki, or if you take the car ferry from Italy to Patras, dual-carriageways *(eTHniki)* run all the way to Athens. Closer to the capital, there are stretches of motorway. Secondary roads are not so good and can often be in quite poor condition. Holders of British driving licences do not need an international driving licence.

The Greek Automobile and Touring Club (ELPA) offers assistance to foreign motorists free of charge if they are members of the AA or RAC. When hiring a car or a motorbike you might find that your passport will be kept until you return. Motorbikes can be hired without a licence.

The rule of the road is: drive on the right, overtake on the left. Priority at cross-roads is as indicated by standard international signs. At cross-roads without road signs, vehicles coming from the right have priority. The speed limit on the national highways is 110 km/h (68 mph), otherwise keep to the speed shown. In built-up areas the limit is 50 km/h (31 mph).

There are plenty of service stations around the main towns. Petrol stations on the highways are usually open 24 hours a day, but elsewhere they close early at night. Fuel rated as 'Super' should be used for all modern cars and large motorbikes, while 'Regular' should be used only for small capacity bikes, or older motors that are better able to cope with lower octane fuel. Greek petrol is the most expensive in Europe. Diesel fuel is about half the price of petrol.

SOME COMMON ROAD SIGNS

αδιέξοδο *athiexotho*	cul-de-sac, dead end
απαγορεύεται η στάθμευση *apagorevete i staTHmefsi*	no parking
γραμμές τραίνου *grames trenoo*	railway crosses road
διαβάση πεζών *thiavasi pezon*	pedestrian crossing
διόδια *thiothia*	toll
έξοδος αυτ/των *exothos aftokiniton*	vehicle exit
έργα *erga*	roadworks
ιδιωτικός δρόμος *ithiotikos thromos*	private road
ισόπεδος διάβασις *isopethos thiavasis*	level crossing, railroad crossing
κέντρο *kedro*	centre
κίνδυνος πυρκαγιάς *kinthinos pirkayas*	fire risk
μονόδρομος *monothromos*	one-way street
νομός *nomos*	county
οδός *othos*	street, road
παραλία *paralia*	beach
πεζοί *pezi*	pedestrians
πρατήριο βενζίνης *pratirio venzinis*	petrol/fuel station
προσοχή *prosohi*	caution
στοπ *'stop'*	stop
σχολείο *s-holio*	school
τέλος *telos*	end
τροχαία *trohea*	traffic police
χιλιόμετρα *hiliometra*	kilometres

USEFUL WORDS AND PHRASES

bonnet	το καπό	*to kapo*
boot	το πορτ-μπαγκάζ	*to port-bagaz*
brake	το φρένο	*to freno*
breakdown	η μηχανική βλάβη	*i mihaniki vlavi*
car	το αυτοκίνητο	*to aftokinito*
caravan	το τροχόσπιτο	*to trohospito*
crossroads	η διασταύρωση	*i thiastavrosi*
to drive	οδηγώ	*othigo*
engine	η μηχανή	*i mihani*
exhaust	η εξάτμιση	*i exatmisi*
fanbelt	το λουρί του βεντιλατέρ	*to loori too ventilater*
garage *(for repairs)*	το συνεργείο	*to sineryio*
(for fuel)	το βενζινάδικο	*to venzinathiko*
gasoline	η βενζίνη	*i venzini*
gear	η ταχύτητα	*i tahitita*
gears	οι ταχύτητες	*i tahitites*
hood *(bonnet)*	το καπό	*to kapo*
junction *(on motorway)*	η έξοδος	*i exothos*
licence	το δίπλωμα	*to thiploma othiyiseos*
lights *(head)*	τα μπροστινά φώτα	*ta brostina fota*
(rear)	τα πίσω φώτα	*ta piso fota*
lorry	το φορτηγό	*to fortigo*
mirror	ο καθρέφτης	*o katHreftis*
motorbike	το μηχανάκι	*to mihanaki*
motorway	η εθνική οδός	*i etHniki othos*
number plate	οι πινακίδες	*i pinakithes*
petrol	η βενζίνη	*i venzini*
road	ο δρόμος	*o thromos*
to skid	γλυστράω	*glistrao*
spares	τα ανταλακτικά	*ta adalaktika*
speed	η ταχύτητα	*i tahitita*
speed limit	το όριο ταχύτητας	*to orio tahititas*
speedometer	το κοντέρ	*to konter*

steering wheel	το τιμόνι	*to timoni*
to tow	τραβάω	*travao*
traffic lights	τα φανάρια	*ta fanaria*
trailer	το ριμουλκό	*to rimoolko*
trailer (R.V.)	το τροχόσπιτο	*to trohospito*
truck	το φορτηγό	*to fortigo*
trunk	το πορτ-μπαγκάζ	*to port-bagaz*
tyre, tire	το λάστιχο	*to lastiho*
van	το φορτηγάκι	*to fortigaki*
wheel	η ρόδα	*i rotha*
windscreen/shield	το μπαρμπρίζ	*to barbriz*

I'd like some petrol (fuel)
Θέλω βενζίνη
THelo venzini

I'd like some oil/water
Θέλω λάδι/νερό
THelo lathi/nero

Fill her up please
Το γεμίζετε, παρακαλώ;
to yemizete, parakalo?

I'd like 10 litres of petrol (fuel)
Θέλω δέκα λίτρα βενζίνη
THelo theka litra venzini

How do I get to...?
Πως μπορώ να πάω...;
pos boro na pao...?

Is this the road to...?
Αυτός είναι ο δρόμος γιά...;
aftos ine o thromos ya...?

Where is the nearest garage?
Που είναι το το πλησιέστερο βενζινάδικο;
poo ine to plisi-estero venzinathiko?

DIRECTIONS YOU MAY BE GIVEN

efτHia	straight on
pernas to/ti...	go past the...
staristera	on the left
sta thexia	on the right
stripse aristera	turn left
stripse thexia	turn right
theftero aristera	second on the left
to proto thexia	first on the right

Would you check the tyres please?
Ελέγχετε τα λάστιχα, παρακαλώ;
elenhete ta lastiha, parakalo?

Do you do repairs?
Κάνετε επισκευές;
kanete episkeves?

Can you repair the clutch?
Μου φτιάχνετε το ντεμπραγιάζ;
moo ftiahnete to debrayaz?

How long will it take?
Πόσο θα κάνει;
poso τHa kani?

There is something wrong with the engine
Κάτι δεν πάει καλά με τη μηχανή
kati then pai kala me ti mihani

29

The engine is overheating
Η μηχανή υπερθερμαίνεται
i mihani iperτHermenete

The brakes are binding
Τα φρένα κολλάνε
ta frena kolane

I need a new tyre
Χρειάζομαι καινούργιο λάστιχο
hriazome kenooryio lastiho

Where can I park?
Που μπορώ να παρκάρω;
poo boro na parkaro?

Can I park here?
Μπορώ να παρκάρω εδώ;
boro na parkaro etho?

I'd like to hire a car
Θέλω να νοικιάσω ένα αυτοκίνητο
τHelo na nikiaso ena aftokinito

THINGS YOU'LL SEE OR HEAR

αεραντλία *aeradlia*	air pump
αλλαγή λαδιών *alayi lathion*	oil change
ανοικτόν *anikton*	open
ανταλλακτικά αυτοκινήτων *adalaktika aftokiniton*	auto spares
αντιπροσωπεία αυτοκινήτων *adiprosopia aftokiniton*	car dealer
αντλία βενζίνης *adlia venzinis*	fuel pump
απλή *apli*	regular

αστυνομία *astinomia*	police
βαφαί αυτοκινήτων *vafe aftokiniton*	automobile paint shop
βενζίνη *venzini*	petrol, gasoline
βουλκανιζατέρ *voolkanizater*	tyre repairs
γκαράζ *garaz*	garage (for parking)
εθνική οδός *ethniki othos*	motorway, highway
ελαστικά *elastika*	tyres, tires
ενοικιάζονται αυτοκίνητα *enikiazode aftokinita*	car rental
εξατμίσεις *exatmisis*	exhausts
έξοδος *exothos*	exit, way out
ηλεκτρολόγος αυτοκινήτων *ilektrologos aftokiniton*	car electrician
λάδια *lathia*	engine oil
σβήστε τη μηχανή *sviste ti mihani*	switch off engine
σούπερ *'super'*	4-star petrol
συνεργείο *sineryio*	auto repairs

RAIL & BOAT TRAVEL

Hellenic Railways Organization [Ο.Σ.Ε.] operates the country's railway network. The trains are modern and maintain regular and comfortable services to the most important regions of the mainland. The network is otherwise not very extensive. There are first and second class season tickets at reduced rates which permit the holder to travel as many times as he wishes. Trains are cheap, a return ticket costing 20% less than two singles. Children aged 14 or under travel at half price.

Boats connect the mainland with all the major islands, and there are frequent ferries to most islands from Piraeus. Altogether there are some 200 ports in the Greek islands and 50 ports on the mainland. The islands are interconnected by sea routes and, for excursions, there are daily around-the-island trips or visits to others nearby.

USEFUL WORDS AND PHRASES

boat	το πλοίο	to plio
booking office	το πρακτορείο	to praktorio
buffet	το μπαρ	to bar
car-ferry	το φέρρυ-μπωτ	to feri-bot
carriage	το βαγόνι	to vagoni
connection	η σύνδεση	i sinthesi
cruise	η κρουαζιέρα	i krooaziera
currency exchange	το συνάλλαγμα	to sinalagma
dining car	η τραπεζαρία του τραίνου	i trapezaria too trenoo
emergency cord	το σήμα κινδύνου	to sima kinthinoo
engine	η μηχανή	i mihani
entrance	η είσοδος	i isothos
exit	η έξοδος	i exothos

ferry	το φέρρυ-μπωτ	*to feri-bot*
first class	η πρώτη θέση	*i proti THesi*
to get in	μπαίνω	*beno*
to get out	βγαίνω	*v-yeno*
hydrofoil	το ιπτάμενο δελφίνι	*to iptameno thelfini*
left luggage	ο χώρος φύλαξης αποσκευών	*o horos filaxis aposkevon*
lost property	τα απολεσθέντα αντικείμενα	*ta apoles-THeda adikimena*
luggage trolley	το καροτσάκι	*to karotsaki*
platform	η πλατφόρμα	*i platforma*
port	το λιμάνι	*to limani*
quay	η προκυμαία	*i prokimea*
rail	οι γραμμές	*i grames*
railway	ο σιδηρόδρομος	*o sithirothromos*
reserved seat	η κλεισμένη θέση	*i klismeni THesi*
restaurant car	το βαγόνι εστιατορίου	*to vagoni estiatorioo*
return ticket	το εισιτήριο μετ'επιστροφής	*to isitirio metepistrofis*
sea	η θάλασσα	*i THalasa*
seat	η θέση	*i THesi*
ship	το πλοίο	*to plio*
station	ο σταθμός	*o staTHmos*
station master	ο σταθμάρχης	*o staTHmarhis*
ticket	το εισιτήριο	*to isitirio*
ticket collector	ο εισπράκτορας	*o ispraktoras*
timetable	τα δρομολόγια	*ta thromoloyia*
train	το τραίνο	*to treno*
waiting room	η αίθουσα αναμονής	*i eTHoosa anamonis*
window	το παράθυρο	*to paraTHiro*

When does the boat for ... leave?
Πότε φεύγει το πλοίο γιά…;
pote fev-yi to plio ya...?

When does the train from ... arrive?
Πότε έρχεται το τραίνο από…;
pote erhete to treno apo...?

When is the next/first/last boat to...?
Πότε είναι το επόμενο/πρώτο/τελευταίο πλοίο γιά…;
pote ine to epomeno/proto/telefteo plio ya...?

What is the fare to...?
Πόσο κάνει το εισιτήριο γιά…;
poso kani to isitirio ya...?

Do I have to change?
Πρέπει ν'αλλάξω;
prepi nalaxo?

Does the boat/train stop at...?
Σταματάει στη…;
stamatai sti...?

How long does it take to get to...?
Πόσες ώρες κάνει να φθάσει…;
poses ores kani na fTHasi...?

A single/return ticket to ... please
Ενα απλό/μετ'επιστροφής εισιτήριο γιά … παρακαλώ
ena aplo/metepistrofis isitirio ya ... parakalo

I'd like to reserve a seat
Θέλω να κλείσω μία θέση
THelo na kliso mia THesi

Is this the right boat for...?
Αυτό είναι το πλοίο γιά...;
afto ine to plio ya...?

Is there a car-ferry to...?
Υπάρχει φέρρυ-μπωτ γιά...;
iparhi feri-bot ya...?

QUESTIONS YOU MAY BE ASKED

Ti aftokinito ine?
What type of car is it?

Ti mikos ehi to aftokinito?
What is the length of your car?

Is this the right platform for the ... train?
Αυτή είναι η σωστή πλατφόρμα γιά το τραίνο προς...;
afti ine i sosti platforma ya to treno pros...?

Which platform for the ... train?
Σε ποιά πλατφόρμα γιά το τραίνο προς...;
se pia platforma ya to treno pros...?

Is the boat late?
Έχει καθυστέρηση το πλοίο;
ehi katHisterisi to plio?

Could you help me with my luggage please?
Μπορείτε να με βοηθήσετε με τις αποσκευές μου,
    παρακαλώ;
borite na me vooiTHisete me tis aposkeves moo, parakalo?

Is this a non-smoking compartment?
Είναι γιά τους μη καπνίζοντες;
ine ya toos mi kapnizodes?

Is this seat free?
Είναι ελεύθερη αυτή η θέση;
ine elefTHeri afti i THesi?

This seat is taken
Αυτή η θέση είναι πιασμένη
afti i THesi ine piasmeni

I have reserved this seat
Έχω κλείσει αυτή τη θέση
eho klisi afti ti THesi

May I open/close the window?
Μπορώ ν'ανοίξω/κλείσω το παράθυρο;
boro nanixo/kliso to paraTHiro?

When do we arrive in...?
Πότε φτάνουμε στο...;
pote ftanoome sto...?

Which island is this?
Ποιό νησί είναι αυτό;
pio nisi ine afto?

Do we stop at...?
Σταματάμε στο...;
stamatame sto...?

Would you keep an eye on my things for a moment?
Μπορείτε να προσέξετε τα πράγματά μου γιά ένα λεπτό;
borite na prosexete ta pragmata moo ya ena lepto?

Is there a restaurant car on this train?
Υπάρχει βαγόνι εστιατορίου σ'αυτό το τραίνο;
iparhi vagoni estiatorioo safto to treno?

THINGS YOU'LL SEE OR HEAR

ακριβές αντίτιμο μόνο	*akrives aditimo mono*	exact fare only
ακτή	*akti*	beach
αριθμός θέσεως	*ariTHmos THeseos*	seat number
αφετηρία	*afetiria*	terminus
διαβατήρια	*thiavatiria*	passports
δρομολόγια	*thromoloyia*	timetable, schedule
εισιτήρια	*isitiria*	tickets
καμπίνες	*kabines*	cabins
καπετάνιος	*kapetanios*	captain
κατάστρωμα	*katastroma*	deck
λέμβος	*lemvos*	lifeboat
λιμενάρχης	*limenarhis*	harbour master
λιμήν	*limin*	port, harbour
λογιστήριο	*loyistirio*	purser's office
Ο/Γ		ferry
ΟΣΕ	*ose*	Hellenic Railways Organisation
προς γκαράζ	*pros garaz*	to car deck
σωσίβια	*sosivia*	life-jackets
τουαλέτες	*tooaletes*	toilets
τραπεζαρία	*trapezaria*	dining room (boat)

AIR TRAVEL

Air services connect Greece with all the major airports of the world. Olympic Airways and many other international airlines provide services to the following Greek destinations: Athens, Thessalonika, and the islands of Corfu, Rhodes, Crete and Mikonos. There is also a large domestic network, operated exclusively by Olympic Airways (O.A.), connecting the main towns, islands and tourist centres. In Athens the Eastern airport serves all foreign airlines, and the Western airport covers all domestic and international O.A. flights.

USEFUL WORDS AND PHRASES

aircraft	το αεροπλάνο	*to aeroplano*
air hostess	η αεροσυνοδός	*i aerosinothos*
airline	οι αερογραμμές	*i aerogrames*
airport	το αεροδρόμιο	*to aerothromio*
airport bus	το λεωφορείο του αεροδρομίου	*to leoforio too aerothromioo*
aisle seat	η θέση δίπλα στο διάδρομο	*i THesi thipla sto thiathromo*
baggage claim	οι αποσκευές	*i aposkeves*
boarding card	η κάρτα αναχώρησης	*i karta anahorisis*
check-in	το τσεκ-ιν	*to 'check-in'*
delay	η καθυστέρηση	*i kaTHisterisi*
departure	η αναχώρηση	*i anahorisi*
departure lounge	η αίθουσα αναχωρήσεων	*i eTHoosa anahoriseon*
emergency exit	η έξοδος κινδύνου	*i exothos kinthinoo*
flight	η πτήση	*i ptisi*
flight number	ο αριθμός πτήσεως	*o ariTHmos ptiseos*
gate	η έξοδος	*i exothos*
jet	το τζετ	*to 'jet'*

38

land	προσγειώνομαι	*prosyionome*
passport	το διαβατήριο	*to thiavatirio*
passport control	ο έλεγχος διαβατηρίων	*o elenhos thiavatirion*
pilot	ο πιλότος	*o pilotos*
runway	ο διάδρομος	*o thiathromos*
seat	η θέση	*i THesi*
seat belt	η ζώνη ασφαλείας	*i zoni asfalias*
steward	ο αεροσυνοδός	*o aerosinothos*
take off	απογειώνομαι	*apoyionome*
window	το παράθυρο	*to paraTHiro*
wing	το φτερό	*to ftero*

When is there a flight to...?
Πότε έχει πτήση γιά...;
pote ehi ptisi ya...?

What time does the flight to ... leave?
Τι ώρα ψεύγει η πτήση γιά...;
ti ora fevyi i ptisi ya...?

Is it a direct flight?
Υπάρχει κατευθείαν πτήση;
iparhi katefTHian ptisi?

Do I have to change planes?
Πρέπει ν'αλλάξω αεροπλάνο;
prepi nalaxo aeroplano?

When do I have to check-in?
Πότε πρέπει να δώσω τις αποσκευές μου;
pote prepi na thoso tis aposkeves moo?

39

I'd like a single/return ticket to...
Θα ήθελα ένα απλό/μετ'επιστροφής εισιτήριο γιά...
THA iTHela ena aplo/metepistrofis isitirio ya...

I'd like a non-smoking seat please
Θέλω μιά θέση στους μη καπνίζοντες, παρακαλώ
THelo mia THesi stoos mi kapnizodes, parakalo

I'd like a window seat please
Θέλω μιά θέση με παράθυρο, παρακαλώ
THelo mia THesi me paraTHiro, parakalo

How long will the flight be delayed?
Πόσο θα καθυστερήσει η πτήση;
poso THA katHisterisi i ptisi?

Is this the right gate for the ... flight?
Αυτή είναι η σωστή έξοδος γιά τη πτήση...;
afti ine i sosti exothos ya ti ptisi...?

When do we arrive in...?
Πότε φτάνουμε...;
pote ftanoome...?

May I smoke now?
Επιτρέπετε να καπνίσω τώρα;
epitrepete na kapniso tora?

I do not feel very well
Δεν αισθάνομαι καλά
THen es-THanome kala

THINGS YOU'LL SEE OR HEAR

O.A. *Olibiaki*	Olympic Airways
αεροδρόμιο *aerothromio*	airport
αερολιμήν *aerolimin*	airport
αεροσυνοδός *aerosinothos*	air hostess
αναχωρήσεις *anahorisis*	departures
απαγορεύεται το κάπνισμα *apagorevete to kapnisma*	no smoking
αφίξεις *afixis*	arrivals
διάδρομος *thiathromos*	runway
διάρκεια πτήσεως *thiarkia ptiseos*	flight time
δρομολόγια *thromoloyia*	timetable
έλεγχος διαβατηρίων *elenhos thiavatirion*	passport control
έξοδος *exothos*	exit, gate, door
έξοδος κινδύνου *exothos kinthinoo*	emergency exit
επιβάτες *epivates*	passengers
κυβερνήτης *kivernitis*	captain
πληροφορίες *plirofories*	information
πλήρωμα *pliroma*	crew
προσδεθήτε *pros-theTHite*	fasten your seat belt
πτήσεις εξωτερικού *ptisis exoterikoo*	international flights
πτήσεις εσωτερικού *ptisis esoterikoo*	domestic flights
τοπική ώρα *topiki ora*	local time
ύψος *ipsos*	altitude

BUS, TAXI & UNDERGROUND TRAVEL

All Greek cities have a good bus network. Most buses are one-man operated and you pay the driver as you enter. In Athens there are electric trolleys in addition to the bus service. In the early morning, from 6 to 8, the bus service is free!

The main towns are connected by an excellent network of long-distance buses, which run punctually and more than make up for the not very extensive railway network. The buses are comfortable, fast and often have air-conditioning. Tickets are bought at the terminus before boarding for the long-distance services.

Taxis are plentiful in Greece, cheaper than in western Europe and used much more frequently. They are yellow or sometimes grey and are marked TAXI. For short local journeys you pay by the kilometre, and the fare is displayed on the meter. For longer drives, ask the fare in advance.

Only Athens has an underground (subway) system, which is called Ο ΗΛΕΚΤΡΙΚΟΣ (o ilektrikos) and which joins Piraeus with Athens and Kifisia.

USEFUL WORDS AND PHRASES

bus	το λεωφορείο	*to leoforio*
bus stop	η στάση	*i stasi*
child	το παιδί	*to pethi*
coach	το πούλμαν	*to poolman*
conductor	ο εισπράκτορας	*o ispraktoras*
connection	η σύνδεση	*i sinthesi*
driver	ο οδηγός	*o othigos*
fare	η τιμή	*i timi*
number five bus	το πέντε	*to pede*
passenger	ο επιβάτης	*o epivatis*
port	το λιμάνι	*to limani*
river	το ποτάμι	*to potami*
sea	η θάλασσα	*i THalasa*

seat	η θέση	*i* THe*si*
station	ο σταθμός	*o sta*THm*os*
taxi	το ταξί	*to taxi*
ticket	το εισιτήριο	*to isitirio*
underground, subway	ο ηλεκτρικός	*o ilektrikos*

Where is the nearest underground station?
Που είναι ο πλησιέστερος σταθμός του ηλεκτρικού;
*poo ine o plisi-esteros sta*THm*os too ilektrikoo?*

Where is the bus station?
Που είναι ο σταθμός των υπεραστικών λεωφορίων;
*poo ine o sta*THm*os ton iperastikon leuforion?*

Where is the bus stop?
Που είναι η στάση;
poo ine i stasi?

Which buses go to...?
Ποιά λεωφορεία πάνε στο...;
pia leoforia pane sto...?

How often do the buses to ... run?
Πόσο συχνά έχει λεωφορείο γιά...;
poso sihna ehi leoforio ya...?

Would you tell me when we get to...?
Μπορείτε να μου πείτε πότε φτάνουμε στο...;
borite na moo pite pote ftanoome sto...?

Do I get off here?
Πρέπει να κατέβω εδώ;
prepi na katevo etho?

How do you get to...?
Πως πάμε στο...;
pos pame sto...?

Is it very far?
Είναι πολύ μακρυά;
ine poli makria?

I want to go to...
Θέλω να πάω στο...
THelo na pao sto...

Do you go near...?
Πάτε κοντά στο...;
pate koda sto...?

Where can I buy a ticket?
Από που μπορώ ν'αγοράσω ένα εισιτήριο;
apo poo boro nagoraso ena isitirio?

Please close/open the window
Παρακαλώ, ανοίγετε/κλείνετε το παράθυρο;
parakalo, aniyete/klinete to paraTHiro?

Could you help me get a ticket?
Μπορείτε να με βοηθήσετε να βγάλω ένα εισιτήριο;
borite na me voiTHisete na vgalo ena isitirio?

When does the last bus leave?
Πότε φεύγει το τελευταίο λεωφορείο;
pote fevyi to telefteo leoforio?

THINGS YOU'LL SEE OR HEAR

απαγορεύεται η είσοδος *apagorevete i isothos*	no entry
γραμμή *grami*	route
εισιτήρια *isitiria*	tickets
έλεγχος εισιτηρίων *elenhos isitirion*	ticket inspection
ελεύθερον *elefTHeron*	free (taxi for hire)
ηλεκτρικός *ilektrikos*	subway, underground
θέσεις *THesis*	seats
μην ομιλείτε στον οδηγό *min omilite ston othigo*	do not speak to the driver
οδηγός *othigos*	driver
ορθίων *orTHion*	standing
παιδικό *pethiko*	children
πρόστιμο *prostimo*	fine (penalty)
πυροσβεστήρ *pirosvestir*	fire extinguisher
σταθμός ταξί *staTHmos taxi*	taxi stand
σταθμός υπεραστικών λεωφορίων *staTHmos iperastikon leoforion*	bus station (long distance)
στάσις *stasis*	bus stop
ταξί *taxi*	taxi
ταρίφα *tarifa*	taxi tariff
χωρητικότητος ... ατόμων *horitikotitos ... atomon*	max load ... persons
χωρίς εισπράκτορα *horis ispraktora*	no ticket collector

RESTAURANT

Restaurants, bars and discos are obliged by law to close at 3.00 am and on Saturday nights at 4.00 am. Children are allowed in places where alcohol is served. Some of the various types of restaurants etc are shown below (notice that signs in Greek capital letters often look different to the same words in 'lower case').

ΕΣΤΙΑΤΟΡΙΟΝ Εστιατόριον *estiatorion*
An ordinary restaurant. In many tourist places you will find the menu printed in English as well as in Greek and the staff will almost certainly speak some English. If you feel more adventurous you might prefer to try some of the many Greek delicacies available, and in smaller establishments you will be welcomed into the kitchen to see what's cooking. In all types of Greek restaurants water and bread come first, without ordering. The menu will usually give you two prices for each item, the first without and the second with service charge.

ΤΑΒΕΡΝΑ Ταβέρνα *taverna*
This is a typical Greek restaurant where draught wine is available. (Note that wine is ordered by weight not by volume, so you'll order a kilo not a litre).

ΨΑΡΟΤΑΒΕΡΝΑ Ψαροταβέρνα *psarotaverna*
A restaurant specializing in seafood.

ΨΗΣΤΑΡΙΑ Ψησταριά *psistaria*
A restaurant specializing in charcoal-grilled food.

ΟΥΖΕΡΙ Ουζερί *oozeri*
A bar which serves ouzo and beer with snacks (called *'mezethes'*) served as side-dishes – these snacks could be savouries or sometimes, and especially in the islands, octopus or local seafood etc.

ΖΑΧΑΡΟΠΛΑΣΤΕΙΟ Ζαχαροπλαστείο *zaharoplastio*
Pastry shop or cafe which serves cakes and soft drinks and is also
an ideal place to have breakfast.

ΚΑΦΕΝΕΙΟ Καφενείο *kafenio*
Coffee house, where Greek coffee is served with traditional sweets
on a spoon. Here you can play a game of cards or backgammon.
Greek women are rarely seen here.

USEFUL WORDS AND PHRASES

beer	η μπύρα	*i bira*
bill	ο λογαριασμός	*o logariasmos*
bottle	το μπουκάλι	*to bookali*
cake	το γλυκό	*to gliko*
chef	ο μάγειρας	*o mayiras*
coffee	ο καφές	*o kafes*
cup	το φλυτζάνι	*to flitzani*
fork	το πηρούνι	*to pirooni*
glass	το ποτήρι	*to potiri*
knife	το μαχαίρι	*to maheri*
menu	το μενού	*to menoo*
milk	το γάλα	*to gala*
plate	το πιάτο	*to piato*
receipt	η απόδειξη	*i apothixi*
sandwich	το σάντουιτς	*to sadooits*
serviette	η χαρτοπετσέτα	*i hartopetseta*
soup	η σούπα	*i soopa*
spoon	το κουτάλι	*to kootali*
sugar	η ζάχαρι	*i zahari*
table	το τραπέζι	*to trapezi*
tea	το τσάι	*to tsai*
teaspoon	το κουταλάκι	*to kootalaki*
tip	το μπουρμπουάρ	*to boorbooar*
waiter	ο σερβιτόρος	*o servitoros*
waitress	η σερβιτόρα	*i servitora*

water	το νερό	*to nero*
wine	το κρασί	*to krasi*
wine list	ο κατάλογος κρασιών	*o katalogos krasion*

A table for 1/2/3 please
Ένα τραπέζι γιά ένα/δύο/τρία άτομα, παρακαλώ
ena trapezi ya ena/thio/tria atoma, parakalo

Can we see the menu/wine list?
Μπορούμε να δούμε το μενού/τον κατάλογο των κρασιών;
boroome na thoome to menoo/ton katalogo ton krasion?

What would you recommend?
Τι θα προτείνατε;
ti THA protinate?

I'd like...
Θα ήθελα...
THA iTHela...

Just a cup of coffee, please
Μόνο ένα φλυτζάνι καφέ, παρακαλώ
mono ena flitzani kafe, parakalo

A kilo/half a kilo of retsina
Ένα κιλό/μισό κιλό ρετσίνα
ena kilo/miso kilo retsina

Waiter!
Γκαρσόν!
garson!

Can we have the bill, please?
Μας φέρνετε τον λογαριασμό, παρακαλώ
mas fernete ton logariasmo, parakalo

I only want a snack
Θέλω κάτι ελαφρύ
THelo kati elafri

I didn't order this
Δεν παράγγειλα αυτό
then paragila afto

May we have some more...?
Μπορούμε να έχουμε ακόμη λίγο...;
boroome na ehoome akomi ligo...?

The meal was very good, thank you
Το φαγητό ήταν πολύ καλό, ευχαριστούμε
to fayito itan poli kalo, efharistoome

My compliments to the chef!
Τα συγχαρητήριά μου στον μάγειρα!
ta sinharitiria moo ston mayira!

MENU GUIDE

αγγινάρες αυγολέμονο *aginares avgolemono* — artichokes in egg and lemon sauce

αγγούρια και ντομάτες σαλάτα *agooria ke domates salata* — cucumber and tomato salad

αλάτι *alati* — salt

αλεύρι καλαμποκιού *alevri kalabokioo* — corn flour

αλεύρι σταριού *alevri starioo* — wheat flour

αλλαντικά *aladika* — sausages, salami, meats

αμύγδαλα *amigthala* — almonds

αμυγδαλωτά *amigthalota* — macaroons

ανανάς *ananas* — pineapple

ανανάς χυμός *ananas himos* — pineapple juice

ανθότυρο *anthotiro* — kind of cottage cheese

αντσούγια στο λάδι *antsooyia sto lathi* — anchovies in oil

αρακάς λαδερός *arakas latheros* — peas cooked with tomato and oil

αρακάς σωτέ *arakas sote* — peas fried in butter

αρνί μπούτι στη λαδόκολα *arni booti sti lathokola* — leg of lamb wrapped in greased foil

αρνί γεμιστό στο φούρνο *arniyemisto sto foorno* — oven-cooked stuffed lamb

αρνί εξοχικό *arni exohiko* — lamb cooked in greased foil with cheese and spices

αρνί κοκκινιστό *arni kokinisto* — lamb in tomato sauce

αρνί λαδορίγανη στο φούρνο *arni lathoriyani sto foorno* — oven-cooked lamb with oil and origano

αρνί με αρακά *arni me araka* — lamb with peas

αρνί με κολοκυθάκια αυγολέμονο *arni me kolokiTHakia avgolemono* — lamb with courgettes in egg and lemon sauce

αρνί με κριθαράκι *arni me kriTHaraki* — lamb with a kind of pasta

αρνί με μελιτζάνες *arni me melitzanes* — lamb with aubergines

αρνί με μπάμιες *arni me bamies* — lamb with okra

αρνί με πατάτες ραγκού *arni me patates ragoo* — lamb with potatoes cooked in tomato sauce αρνί με φασολάκια φρέσκα *arni me fasolakia freska* — lamb with runner beans

αρνί με χυλοπίτες *arni me hilopites* — lamb with a kind of lasagne

αρνί μπούτι στο φούρνο *arni booti sto foorno* — oven-cooked leg of lamb

αρνί μπριζόλες *arni brizoles* — lamb chops

αρνί με μακαρόνια *arni me makaronia* — lamb with spaghetti

αρνί παϊδάκια *arni paithakia* — grilled lamb chops

αρνί τας κεμπάπ *arni tas kebab* — chopped lamb kebab with tomato sauce

αρνί της κατσαρόλας με πατάτες *arni tis katsarolas me patates* — casseroled lamb with potatoes

αρνί της σούβλας *arni tis soovlas* — spit-roast lamb

αρνί φρικασέ *arni frikase* — lamb fricassée

αστακός με λαδολέμονο *astakos me latholemono* — lobster cooked in lemon and oil sauce

αστακός με μαγιονέζα *astakos me mayoneza* — lobster with mayonnaise

αστακός βραστός *astakos vrastos* — boiled lobster

ατζέμ πιλάφι *atzem pilafi* — rice pilaf

αυγά βραστά *avga vrasta* — boiled eggs

αυγά βραστά σφιχτά *avga vrasta sfihta* — hard-boiled eggs

αυγά γεμιστά *avga yemista* — stuffed eggs

αυγά γεμιστά με μαγιονέζα *avga yemista me mayoneza* — stuffed eggs with mayonnaise

αυγά μάτια *avga matia* — fried eggs

αυγά με μανιτάρια *avga me manitaria* — mushroom omelette

αυγά με μπέικον *avga me 'bacon'* — bacon and eggs

αυγά με ντομάτες *avga me domates* — eggs cooked in tomato sauce

αυγά με τυρί *avga me tiri* — cheese omelette

αυγά ομελέτα *avga omeleta* — plain omelette

αυγά ομελέτα με πατάτες *avga omeleta me patates* — omelette with chips

αυγά ποσέ *avga pose* — poached eggs

αυγά ω γκρατέν *avga o graten* — eggs au gratin

αυγολέμονο σούπα *avgolemono soopa* — egg and lemon soup

αυγοτάραχο *avgotaraho* — roe

51

αχλάδι χυμός	*ahlathi himos*	pear juice
αχλάδια	*ahlathia*	pears
βακαλάος κροκέτες	*vakalaos kroketes*	haddock croquettes
βερύκοκκα τάρτα	*verikoka tarta*	apricot tart
βερύκοκκα χυμός	*verikoka himos*	apricot juice
βερύκοκκα	*verikoka*	apricots
βούτυρο	*vootiro*	butter
βούτυρο φυστικιού	*vootiro fistikioo*	peanut butter
βρασμένος	*vrasmenos*	boiled
βυσσινάδα	*visinatha*	black cherry juice
βύσσινο	*visino*	sour cherries
βωδινό βραστό	*vothino vrasto*	boiled beef
βωδινό ροσμπίφ	*vothino rosbif*	roast beef
βωδινό φιλέτο σχάρα	*vothino fileto s-hara*	grilled beef steak
βωδινό ψητό στο φούρνο	*vothino psito sto foorno*	roast beef cooked in the oven
βωδινός κιμάς	*vothinos kimas*	minced beef
βωδινό κορν-μπίφ	*vothino korn-bif*	corned beef
γάβρος στο φούρνο με ντομάτα	*gavros sto foorno me domata*	small type of fish cooked in the oven with tomato sauce
γάβρος τηγανητός	*gavros tiganitos*	fried small fish
γάλα	*gala*	milk
γάλα αγελάδος με λίπος 1%	*gala ayelathos me lipos ena tis ekato*	cow's milk with 1% fat
γάλα εβαπορέ	*gala evapore*	evaporated milk
γάλα σοκολατούχο	*gala sokolatooho*	chocolate milk
γάλα συμπηκνωμένο ζαχαρούχο	*gala sibiknomeno zaharooho*	sweet evaporated milk
γαλακτομπούρεκο	*galaktobooreko*	cream pie with honey
γαλέος τηγανητός σκορδαλιά	*galeos tiganitos skorthalia*	fried cod with garlic sauce
γαλλικός καφές	*galikos kafes*	French coffee
γαλοπούλα ψητή στο φούρνο	*galopoola psiti sto foorno*	roast turkey
γαλοπούλα γεμιστή	*galopoola yemisti*	stuffed turkey
γαλοπούλα κοκκινιστή	*galopoola*	turkey cooked with

kokinisti	tomatoes
γαρίδες **κανапέ** *garithes kanape*	shrimp canapés
γαρδούμπα *garthooba*	lamb's intestines on the spit
γαρίδες βραστές *garithes vrastes*	boiled shrimps
γαρίδες **κοκτέιλ** *garithes 'cocktail'*	shrimp cocktail
γαρίδες πιλάφι *garithes pilafi*	shrimp pilaf
γαρνιτούρα **καρότα** σωτέ *garnitoora karota sote*	sautéed carrots
γαρνιτούρα **κουνουπίδι** σωτέ *garnitoora koonoopithi sote*	sautéed cauliflower
γαρνιτούρα πατάτες *garnitoora patates*	potatoes
γαρνιτούρα σπανάκι σωτέ *garnitoora spanaki sote*	sautéed spinach
γαρνιτούρα φασόλια πράσινα σωτέ *garnitoora fasolia prasina sote*	sautéed runner beans
γαρνιτούρα φασόλια ξερά σωτέ *garnitoora fasolia xera sote*	sautéed butter beans
γιαλαντζή ντολμάδες *yalantzi dolmathes*	vine leaves stuffed with rice
γιαούρτι αγελάδος άπαχο *yaoorti ayelathos apaho*	cow's yoghurt (low fat)
γιαούρτι αγελάδος πλήρες *yaoorti ayelathos plires*	cow's yoghurt (with fat)
γιαούρτι πρόβειο *yaoorti provio*	sheep's yoghurt
γιαούρτι φρούτων *yaoorti frooton*	fruit yoghurt
γιουβαρλάκια αυγολέμονο *yioovarlakia avgolemono*	meatballs with rice in egg and lemon sauce
γιουβαρλάκια με σάλτσα ντομάτας *yioovarlakia me saltsa domatas*	meatballs with rice cooked with tomatoes
γιουβέτσι *yoovetsi*	oven-cooked lamb with a kind of pasta
γκοφρέττα *gofreta*	chocolate wafer
γκρέϊπ φρουτ χυμός *'grapefruit' himos*	grapefruit juice
γκρκρέϊπ φρουτ *'grapefruit'*	grapefruit
γλυκό μελιτζανάκι *gliko melitzanaki*	dried small aubergine in syrup
γλυκό βύσσινο *gliko visino*	dried cherry in syrup
γλυκό **καρυδάκι** φρέσκο *gliko*	dried fresh green walnut in

53

karithaki fresko	syrup
γλυκό μαστίχα *gliko mastiha*	vanilla-flavoured fudge
γλυκό νεραντζάκι *gliko nerantzaki*	dried bitter orange in syrup
γλυκό σύκο φρέσκο *gliko siko fresko*	dried fig in syrup
γλυκό τριαντάφυλλο *gliko triadafilo*	dried rose petals in syrup
γλώσσες *gloses*	sole
γλώσσες τηγανητές *gloses tiganites*	fried sole
γόπα τηγανητή *gopa tiganiti*	type of fried fish
γουρουνόπουλο στο φούρνο με πατάτες *gooroonopoolo sto foorno me patates*	oven-cooked pork with potatoes
γραβιέρα τυρί *graviera tiri*	kind of savoury cheese
γρανίτα λεμόνι *granita lemoni*	lemon sorbet
γρανίτα μπανάνα *granita banana*	banana sorbet
γρανίτα πορτοκάλι *granita portokali*	orange sorbet
γρανίτα φράουλες *granita fraooles*	strawberry sorbet
δαμάσκηνα *thamaskina*	prunes
δίπλες *thiples*	pancakes
εκλαίρ σοκολάτας *ekler sokolatas*	chocolate éclair
εκμέκ κατάιφι *ekmek kataifi*	sweet with nuts, honey and cream
ελαιόλαδο *eleolatho*	olive oil
ελιές *elies*	olives
ελληνικός καφές *elinikos kafes*	Greek coffee
εντόστια αρνιού λαδορίγανη *entostia arnioo lathorigani*	lambs' intestines cooked in lemon and oil
εσκαλόπ με ζαμπόν και σάλτσα ντομάτας *eskalop me zabon ke saltsa domatas*	escalope of veal with ham and tomato sauce
ζαμπόν *zabon*	ham
ζάχαρη μαύρη *zahari mavri*	brown sugar
ζάχαρη άσπρη *zahari aspri*	white sugar
ζελέ βερύκοκκου *zele verikokoo*	apricot jelly
ζελέ κεράσι *zele kerasi*	cherry jelly
ζελέ πορτοκαλιού *zele portokalioo*	orange jelly
ζελέ φράουλα *zele fraoola*	strawberry jelly
ζυμαρικά *zimarika*	pasta
ζωμός κότας/κρέατος/λαχανικών	chicken/beef/vegetable

zomos kotas/kreatos/lahanikon	stock
ηλιέλαιο *ilieleo*	sunflower oil
θαλασσινά *THalasina*	sea fish
καβούρια ψητά *kavooria psita*	grilled crabs
κακαβιά ψαρόσουπα *kakavia psarosoopa*	fish soup
κακάο *kakao*	cocoa
κακάο ρόφημα *kakao rofima*	hot chocolate
καλαμαράκια γεμιστά *kalamarakia yemista*	stuffed squid
καλαμαράκια τηγανητά *kalamarakia tiganita*	fried squid
καλαμποκέλαιο *kalabokeleo*	corn oil
καλαμπόκι *kalaboki*	corn
καναπέ με ζαμπόν *kanape me zabon*	ham canapés
καναπέ με κρέας ψητό *kanape me kreas psito*	cooked meat canapés
καναπέ με μαύρο χαβιάρι *kanape me mavro huviari*	black caviar canapés
καναπέ με ταραμοσαλάτα *kanape me taramosalata*	taramosalata canapés
κανελλόνια γεμιστά *kanelonia yemista*	stuffed canelloni
καπαμάς αρνί *kapamas arni*	lamb cooked in spices and tomato sauce
καραβίδες *karavithes*	prawns
καραμέλες *karameles*	candies
καρμπονάρα *karbonara*	spaghetti carbonara
καρότα *karota*	carrots
καρπούζι *karpoozi*	water melon
καρύδα *karitha*	coconut
καρύδια *karithia*	walnuts
καρυδόπιττα *karithopita*	cake with nuts and syrup
κασέρι *kaseri*	type of Greek cheese
κάστανα *kastana*	chestnuts
κάστανα γλασέ *kastana glase*	glazed chestnuts
καταΐφι *kataifi*	sweet with honey and nuts
καφές βαρύς γλυκός *kafes varis glikos*	sweet Greek coffee

καφές με γάλα *kafes me gala*	coffee with milk
καφές μέτριος *kafes metrios*	medium sweet Greek coffee
κέϊκ κανέλλας *'cake' kanelas*	cinnamon cake
κέϊκ με αμύγδαλα *'cake' me amigthala*	almond cake
κέϊκ με καρύδια και σταφίδες *'cake' me karithia ke stafithes*	nut and sultana cake
κέϊκ σοκολάτας *'cake' sokolatas*	chocolate cake
κέϊκ φρούτων *'cake' frooton*	fruit cake
κεράσια *kerasia*	cherries
κετσάπ *'ketchup'*	ketchup
κέφαλος *kefalos*	mullet
κεφαλοτύρι *kefalotiri*	type of Greek parmesan cheese
κεφτέδες τηγανητοί *keftethes tiganiti*	fried meatballs
κεφτέδες με σάλτσα *keftethes me saltsa*	meatballs in tomato sauce
κεφτέδες στο φούρνο *keftethes sto foorno*	oven-cooked meatballs
κόκα κόλα *kokakola*	coke
κοκορέτσι *kokoretsi*	spit-roast lambs' intestines
κολιοί ψητοί *koli-i psiti*	fried mackerel
κολοκυθάκια γεμιστά με ρύζι *kolokiтнakia yemista me rizi*	courgettes stuffed with rice
κολοκυθάκια λαδερά *kolokiтнakia lathera*	courgettes cooked in oil
κολοκυθάκια σαλάτα *kolokiтнakia salata*	courgette salad
κολοκυθάκια τηγανητά *kolokiтнakia tiganita*	fried courgettes
κολοκυθοκεφτέδες *kolokiтнokeftethes*	fried courgette balls
κολοκυθοτυρόπιττα *kolokiтнotiropita*	courgette and cheese pie
κολοκυθάκια γεμιστά με κιμά *kolokiтнakia yemista me kima*	courgettes stuffed with minced meat
κολοκυθάκια με πατάτες *kolokiтнakia me patates*	courgettes with potatoes
κολοκυθάκια μουσακάς *kolokiтнakia moosakas*	courgettes with minced meat and béchamel sauce
κολοκυθάκια παπουτσάκι	courgettes with minced meat

kolokiтнakia papootsaki	and onions
κομπόστα βερύκοκκα *kobosta verikoka*	apricot compôte
κομπόστα μήλα *kobosta mila*	apple compôte
κομπόστα ροδάκινα *kobosta rothakina*	peach compôte
κορν φλέϊκς *'corn flakes'*	corn flakes
κότα βραστή *kota vrasti*	boiled chicken
κότα γεμιστή *kota yemisti*	stuffed chicken
κότα κοκκινιστή *kota kokinisti*	chicken in tomato sauce
κότα ψητή στο φούρνο *kota psiti sto foorno*	roast chicken
κότα ψητή σούβλας *kota psiti soovlas*	spit-roast chicken
κότα ψητή της κατσαρόλας *kota psiti tis katsarolas*	roast chicken in the pot
κοτολέτες αρνίσιες πανέ *kotoletes arnisies pane*	lamb cutlets
κοτολέτες μοσχαρίσιες πανέ *kotoletes mosharisies pane*	veal cutlets
κοτόπιττα *kotopita*	chicken pie
κοτόπουλο γιουβέτσι με χυλοπίττες *kotopoolo yioovetsi me hilopites*	chicken with a kind of pasta
κοτόπουλο με μπάμιες *kotopoolo me bamies*	chicken with okra
κοτόπουλο με μπιζέλια *kotopoolo me bizelia*	chicken with peas
κοτόπουλο πανέ *kotopoolo pane*	breaded chicken
κοτόπουλο πιλάφι *kotopoolo pilafi*	chicken pilaf
κοτόσουπα *kotosoopa*	chicken soup
κουκιά λαδερά *kookia lathera*	broad beans in tomato sauce
κουλούρια κανέλας/σουσάμι *koolooria kanelas/soosami*	cinnamon/sesame biscuits
κουνέλι με σάλτσα *kooneli me saltsa*	rabbit with tomato sauce
κουνέλι στιφάδο *kooneli stifatho*	rabbit with onions
κουνουπίδι βραστό σαλάτα *koonoopithi vrasto salata*	boiled cauliflower salad
κουραμπιέδες με αμύγδαλο *koorabiethes me amigthalo*	shortbread with icing sugar

κράκερς αλμυρά	*krakers almira*	salted crackers
κρασί	*krasi*	wine
κρασί άσπρο	*krasi aspro*	white wine
κρασί κόκκινο	*krasi kokino*	red wine
κρασί μαυροδάφνη	*krasi mavrothafni*	sweet red wine
κρασί ρετσίνα	*krasi retsina*	dry white Greek wine
κρασί ροζέ	*krasi roze*	rosé wine
κρέας με αντίδια αυγολέμονο	*kreas me antithia avgolemono*	beef with endives in egg and lemon sauce
κρέας με φασόλια ξερά	*kreas me fasolia xera*	beef with butter beans
κρεατόπιττες	*kreatopites*	minced meat pies
κρέμα καραμελέ	*krema karamele*	crème caramel
κρέμα με μήλα	*krema me mila*	apples with cream
κρέμα με μπανάνες	*krema me bananes*	bananas with cream
κρεμμυδάκια φρέσκα	*kremithakia freska*	spring onions
κρεμμύδια	*kremithia*	onions
κρεμμυδόσουπα	*kremithosoopa*	onion soup
κροκέτες από κρέας	*kroketes apo kreas*	meat croquettes
κροκέτες με αυγά και τυρί	*kroketes me avga ke tiri*	croquettes with egg and cheese
κροκέτες μπακαλιάρου	*kroketes bakaliaroo*	cod croquettes
κροκέτες πατάτες	*kroketes patates*	potato croquettes
κρουασάν	*'croissants'*	croissants
κυδωνόπαστο	*kithonopasto*	thick quince jelly
κωκ	*kok*	cake with cream and chocolate topping
λαγός με σάλτσα	*lagos me saltsa*	hare in tomato sauce
λαγός στιφάδο	*lagos stifatho*	hare with onions
λάδι	*lathi*	oil
λαζάνια	*lazania*	lasagne
λαχανάκια Βρυξελλών	*lahanakia vrixelon*	Brussels sprouts
λαχανικά μικτά	*lahanika mikta*	mixed vegetables

λάχανο *lahano*	cabbage
λάχανο κόκκινο *lahano kokino*	red cabbage
λάχανο ντολμάδες αυγολέμονο *lahano dolmathes avgolemono*	cabbage leaves stuffed with rice in egg and lemon sauce
λάχανο ντολμάδες με σάλτσα ντομάτας *lahano dolmathes me saltsa domatas*	vine leaves stuffed with rice in tomato sauce
λαχανοσαλάτα *lahanosalata*	cabbage salad
λεμονάδα *lemonatha*	lemonade
λεμόνι *lemoni*	lemon
λεμόνι χυμός *lemoni himos*	lemon juice
λιθρίνι ψητό *liTHrini psito*	grilled mullet
λουκάνικα βραστά *lookanika vrasta*	boiled sausages
λουκάνικα καπνιστά στη σχάρα *lookanika kapnista sti s-hara*	smoked sausages from the grill
λουκάνικα τηγανητά *lookanika tiganita*	fried sausages
λουκουμάδες *lookoomathes*	doughnuts
λουκούμια *lookoomia*	Turkish delight
μαγειρίτσα *mayiritsa*	Easter soup with lambs' intestines
μαγιά *mayia*	yeast
μαγιονέζα *mayoneza*	mayonnaise
μαϊντανός *maidanos*	parsley
μακαρονάκι κοφτό *makaronaki kofto*	macaroni
μακαρόνια με κιμά *makaronia me kima*	spaghetti bolognaise
μακαρόνια με φρέσκο βούτυρο και παρμεζάνα *makaronia me fresko vootiro ke parmezana*	spaghetti with fresh butter and parmesan cheese
μακαρόνια παστίτσιο με κιμά *makaronia pastitsio me kima*	spaghetti with rice and béchamel sauce
μανιτάρια *manitaria*	mushrooms
μανιτάρια τηγανητά *manitaria tiganita*	fried mushrooms
μανταρίνι *madarini*	tangerine
μαργαρίνη *margarini*	margarine
μαρίδες τηγανητές *marithes tiganites*	small fried fish
μαρμελάδα βερύκοκκο *marmelatha verikoko*	apricot jam
μαρμελάδα πορτοκάλι *marmelatha*	orange jam

portokali

μαρμελάδα ροδάκινο *marmelatha pothakino*		peach jam
μαρμελάδα φράουλες *marmelatha fraooles*		strawberry jam
μαρούλια σαλάτα *maroolia salata*		lettuce salad
μέλι *meli*		honey
μελιτζάνες γιαχνί *melitzanes yahni*		aubergines in tomato and onions
μελιτζάνες παπουτσάκι *melitzanes papootsaki*		aubergines cooked with minced meat and tomato
μελιτζάνες γεμιστές με κιμά *melitzanes gemistes me kima*		aubergines stuffed with minced meat
μελιτζάνες ιμάμ μπαϊλντί *melitzanes imam baildi*		aubergines in garlic and tomato
μελιτζάνες μουσακάς *melitzanes moosakas*		aubergines in minced meat, meat, potato and béchamel sauce
μελιτζάνες τηγανητές *melitzanes tiganites*		fried aubergines
μελιτζανοσαλάτα *melitzanosalata*		aubergine salad
μελομακάρονα *melomakarona*		sweet cakes with cinnamon, nuts and syrup
μήλα *mila*		apples
μήλα γεμιστά *mila yemista*		stuffed apples with cinnamon
μηλόπιττα *milopita*		apple pie
μηλοχυμός *milohimos*		apple juice
μοσχάρι βραστό *mos-hari vrasto*		veal stew
μοσχάρι κοκκινιστό *mos-hari kokinisto*	veal in tomato sauce
μοσχάρι με κριθαράκι *mos-hari me kritHaraki*		veal with a kind of lasagne
μοσχάρι με μελιτζάνες *mos-hari me melitzanes*		veal with aubergines
μοσχάρι με μπάμιες *mos-hari me bamies*		veal with okra
μοσχάρι με πατάτες *mos-hari me patates*	veal with potatoes

μοσχάρι με πατάτες στο φούρνο *mos-hari me patates sto foorno* — veal with potatoes cooked in the oven

μοσχάρι με πουρέ *mos-hari me poore* — veal with mashed potatoes

μοσχάρι ροσμπίφ *mos-hari rosbif* — roast beef

μοσχάρι με αρακά *mos-hari me araka* — veal with peas

μοσχάρι σνίτζελ με πατάτες τηγανητές *mos-hari 'schnitzel' me patates tiganites* — steak and chips

μοσχάρι σνίτζελ με πουρέ *mos-hari 'schnitzel' me poore* — steak with mashed potatoes

μοσχαρίσιος κιμάς *mos-harisios kimas* — minced meat

μουσακάς *moosakas* — moussaka

μουσακάς πατάτες *moosakas patates* — potatoes with minced meat and béchamel sauce

μουστοκούλουρα *moostokooloora* — kind of Greek biscuits

μουστάρδα *moostartha* — mustard

μπακαλιάρος πλακί *bakaliaros plaki* — salted cod cooked in tomato sauce

μπακαλιάρος τηγανητός *bakaliaros tiganitos* — fried salted cod

μπακλαβάδες με καρύδια *baklavathes me karithia* — baclava: pastry layered with walnuts and syrup

μπάμιες λαδερές *bamies latheres* — okra with tomato in oil

μπανάνα *banana* — banana

μπαρμπούνια πανέ *barboonia pane* — breaded red mullet

μπεζέδες *bezethes* — meringues with cream

μπέικον καπνιστό *'bacon' kapnisto* — smoked bacon

μπεσαμέλ σάλτσα *besamel saltsa* — béchamel sauce

μπισκότα σοκολάτας *biskota sokolatas* — chocolate biscuits

μπισκοτάκια αλμυρά *biskotakia almira* — savoury crackers

μπιφτέκι *bifteki* — grilled meatballs

μπον φιλέ *bon file* — fillet steak

μπουγάτσα γλυκιά *boogatsa glikia* — puff pastry with creamy filling and icing sugar

μπουρεκάκια *boorekakia* — cheese pies

μπριάμι με κολοκυθάκια *briami me kolokithakia* — courgettes cooked with potatoes in the oven

μπριζόλες βωδινές στη σχάρα *brizoles* — grilled T-bone steak

vothines sti s-hara	
μπριζόλες στο τηγάνι *brizoles sto tigani*	fried T-bone steak
μπριζόλες χοιρινές *brizoles hirines*	pork chops
μπρόκολο *brokolo*	broccoli
μπύρα *bira*	beer
μυαλά πανέ *miala pane*	breaded beef brains
μύδια τηγανητά *mithia tiganita*	fried mussels
νες καφέ *neskafe*	any 'instant' coffee
νεφρά ψητά/τηγανητά *nefra psita/ tiganita*	grilled/fried kidneys
ντολμάδες αυγολέμονο με κιμά *dolmathes avgolemono me kima*	vine leaves with rice and mince in egg lemon sauce
ντολμάδες γιαλαντζή *dolmathes yialantzi*	stuffed vine leaves with rice
ντοματόσουπα *domatosoopa*	tomato soup
ντομάτα χυμός *domata himos*	tomato juice
ντομάτες γεμιστές με κιμά *domates yemistes me kima*	stuffed tomatoes with mince
ντοματοσαλάτα *domatosalata*	tomato salad
ντομάτα *domata*	tomato
ντομάτες γεμιστές με ρύζι *domates yemistes me rizi*	stuffed tomatoes with rice
ντόνατς *'doughnuts'*	doughnuts
ξηροί καρποί *xiri karpi*	all kinds of nuts
ξιφίας *xifias*	sword fish
ξύδι *xithi*	vinegar
ομελέτα *omeleta*	omelette
ομελέτα λουκάνικα *omeleta lookanika*	omelette with sausages
ορεκτικά *orektika*	hors d'oeuvres
ούζο *oozo*	ouzo
παγωτό κοκτέηλ *pagoto 'cocktail'*	ice cream cocktail
παγωτό κρέμα *pagoto krema*	vanilla ice cream
παγωτό βερύκοκκο *pagoto verikoko*	apricot ice cream
παγωτό με σαντιγύ *pagoto me sadiyi*	ice cream with whipped cream
παγωτό μόκκα *pagoto moka*	coffee ice cream
παγωτό μπανάνα *pagoto banana*	banana ice cream

παγωτό παρφαί	*pagoto parfe*	ice cream parfait
παγωτό πραλίνα	*pagoto pralina*	praline ice cream
παγωτό σοκολάτα	*pagoto sokolata*	chocolate ice cream
παγωτό φράουλα	*pagoto fraoola*	strawberry ice cream
παγωτό φυστίκι	*pagoto fistiki*	pistachio ice cream
πάπρικα	*paprika*	paprika
πάστα αμυγδάλου	*pasta amigthaloo*	almond gateau
πάστα κορμός	*pasta kormos*	chocolate log
πάστα νουγκατίν	*pasta noogatin*	cream gateau
πάστα σοκολατίνα	*pasta sokolatina*	chocolate gateau
πάστα φράουλα	*pasta fraoola*	strawberry gateau
παστίτσιο λαζάνια	*pastitsio lazania*	lasagne
παστίτσιο μακαρόνια με κιμά	*pastitsio makaronia me kima*	spaghetti with mince in a pie form
πατάτες γαρνιτούρα	*patates garnitoora*	potatoes
πατάτες γιαχνί	*patates yahni*	potatoes cooked with onion and tomato
πατάτες και κολοκυθάκια στο φούρνο	*patates ke kolokithakia sto foorno*	potatoes, courgettes and tomatoes cooked in the oven
πατάτες κολοκύθια μουσακάς	*patates kolokithia moosakas*	potatoes with courgettes, mince and cheese sauce
πατάτες πουρέ	*patates poore*	mashed potatoes
πατάτες σουφλέ	*patates soofle*	potato soufflé
πατάτες στο φούρνο ριγανάτες	*patates sto foorno riganates*	potatoes baked in the oven with origano, lemon and olive oil
πατάτες τηγανιτές	*patates tiganites*	French fries/chips
πατάτες τσιπς	*patates tsips*	potato crisps
πατατοσαλάτα	*patatosalata*	potato salad
πατζάρια	*patzaria*	beetroots
πατσάς σούπα	*patsas soopa*	tripe
πεπόνι	*peponi*	melon
πέστροφα ψητή	*pestrofa psiti*	grilled trout
πηχτή	*pihti*	potted meat
πιλάφι με γαρίδες	*pilafi me garithes*	shrimp pilaf
πιλάφι με μύδια	*pilafi me mithia*	rice with mussels

πιλάφι με σάλτσα ντομάτα *pilafi me saltsa domata*	rice with tomato sauce
πιλάφι τας-κεμπάπ *pilafi tas kebab*	rice with cubes of beef in tomato sauce
πιπέρι *piperi*	pepper
πιπεριές γεμιστές με ρύζι/κιμά *piperies yemistes me rizi/kima*	stuffed peppers with rice/mince
πιπεριές πράσινες/κόκκινες *piperies prasines/kokines*	green/red peppers
πιπεριές τηγανητές *piperies tiganites*	fried peppers
πιροσκί *piroski*	mince or sausage rolls
πίτσα με ζαμπόν *'pizza' me zabon*	ham pizza
πίτσα με μανιτάρια *'pizza' me manitaria*	mushroom pizza
πίτσα με ντομάτα τυρί *'pizza' me domata tiri*	cheese and tomato pizza
πίτσα σπέσιαλ *'pizza' special*	special pizza
πίττα με κιμά *pita me kima*	minced meat pie
πορτοκαλάδα *portokalatha*	orange juice
πορτοκάλι *portokali*	orange
πορτοκάλι χυμός *portokali himos*	orange juice
πουτίγκα με ανανά *pootiga me anana*	pineapple pudding
πουτίγκα με καρύδια *pootiga me karithia*	pudding with walnuts
πουτίγκα με σταφίδες *pootiga me stafithes*	sultana pudding
πρασσόπιττα *prasopita*	leek pie
πράσσα *prasa*	leeks
παρμεζάνα *parmezana*	parmesan cheese
ραβιόλια *raviolia*	ravioli
ραβανί *ravani*	very sweet sponge cake
ρίγανη *rigani*	oregano
ροδάκινα *rothakina*	peaches
ροσμπίφ αρνί μοσχάρι *rozbif arni mos-hari*	roast beef, veal or lamb
ρυζόγαλο *rizogalo*	rice pudding
ρωσική σαλάτα *rosiki salata*	vegetable salad
σαλάτα αμπελοφάσουλα *salata*	runner bean salad

abelofasoola

σαλάτα μαρούλια	*salata maroolia*	lettuce salad
σαλάτα ντομάτες και αγγούρια	*salata domates ke ugooria*	tomato and cucumber salad
σαλάτα σπαράγγια	*salata sparagia*	asparagus salad
σαλάμι	*salami*	salami
σαλάτα	*salata*	salad
σαλάτα κουνουπίδι βραστό	*salata koonoopithi vrasto*	boiled cauliflower salad
σαλάτα ντομάτες-πιπεριές	*salata domates piperies*	tomato and green pepper salad
σαλάτα φασόλια ξερά	*salata fasolia xera*	butter bean salad
σαλάτα χόρτα βρασμένα	*salata horta vrasmena*	chicory salad
σαλάτα χωριάτικη	*salata horiatiki*	Greek salad – tomatoes, cucumber, feta cheese, peppers and olives
σαλιγκάρια	*saligaria*	snails
σάλτσα μπεσαμέλ	*saltsa besamel*	béchamel sauce
σάλτσα ντομάτα	*saltsa domata*	tomato sauce
σάμαλι	*samali*	semolina cake with honey
σαντιγύ	*sadiyi*	whipped cream
σαρδέλλες λαδιού	*sartheles lathioo*	sardines in oil
σέλινο	*selino*	celery
σιμιγδάλι	*simigthali*	semolina
σιρόπι	*siropi*	syrup
σκορδαλιά με ψωμί	*skorthalia me psomi*	thick garlic sauce with bread
σκόρδο	*skortho*	garlic
σοκολάτα	*sokolata*	chocolate
σοκολατάκια	*sokolatakia*	milk chocolates
σολομός καπνιστός	*solomos kapnistos*	smoked salmon
σουβλάκι καλαμάκι	*soovlaki kalamaki*	shish kebab
σουβλάκι ντονέρ με πίττα	*soovlaki doner me pita*	donner kebab with pitta bread
σουβλάκια από κρέας μοσχαρίσιο		veal kebab

soovlakia apo kreas mos-harisio

σουβλάκια από κρέας αρνίσιο *soovlakia apo kreas arnisio*	lamb kebab
σουβλάκια από κρέας χοιρινό *soovlakia apo kreas hirino*	pork kebab
σούπα ρεβύθια *soopa reviᴛʜia*	chickpea soup
σούπα τραχανάς *soopa trahanas*	milk broth with flour
σούπα φακές *soopa fakes*	lentil soup
σούπα ψάρι/ψαρόσουπα αυγολέμονο *soopa psari/psarosoopa avgolemono*	fish soup with egg and lemon
σουπιές τηγανητές *soopies tiganites*	fried cuttlefish
σουσάμι *soosami*	sesame
σουτζουκάκια *sootzookakia*	spicy meatballs in red sauce
σουφλέ με ζαμπόν *soofle me zabon*	ham soufflé
σουφλέ τυριού *soofle tirioo*	cheese soufflé
σπαγέτο με φρέσκο βούτυρο και παρμεζάνα *spageto me fresko vootiro ke parmezana*	spaghetti with fresh butter and parmesan cheese
σπαράγγια σαλάτα *sparagia salata*	asparagus salad
σπληνάντερο *splinadero*	intestines stuffed with spleen
σταφίδες *stafithes*	raisins
σταφιδόψωμο *stafithopsomo*	bread with raisins
σταφύλι χυμός *stafili himos*	grape juice
σταφύλια *stafilia*	grapes
στιφάδο *stifatho*	chopped meat in onions
στρείδια *strithia*	oysters
σύκα *sika*	figs
συκωτάκια μαρινάτα *sikotakia marinata*	liver cooked in rosemary
συκωτάκια πιλάφι *sikotakia pilafi*	liver pilaf
συκωτάκια στη σχάρα *sikotakia sti s-hara*	grilled liver
συκωτάκια τηγανητά *sikotakia tiganita*	fried liver
συναγρίδα ψητή *sinagritha psiti*	grilled sea-bream
σφυρίδα βραστή *sfiritha vrasti*	boiled pike
ταραμοκεφτέδες *taramokeftethes*	roe pâté balls with spices
ταραμοσαλάτα *taramosalata*	roe pâté

τάρτα με κεράσια *tarta me kerasia*	cherry tart
τάρτα με κρέμα και αμύγδαλα *tarta me krema ke amigthala*	cream and almond tart
τάρτα με κρέμα και καρύδια *tarta me krema ke karithia*	cream and walnut tart
τάρτα με φράουλες *tarta me fraooles*	strawberry tart
τάρτα μήλου *tarta miloo*	apple tart
τας-κεμπάπ *tas kebab*	spicy lamb cutlets
τας-κεμπάπ πιλάφι *tas kebab pilafi*	spicy lamb cutlets pilaf
τζατζίκι *tzatziki*	yoghurt, cucumber, garlic and oil
τηγανητός *tiganitos*	fried
τηγανίτες *tiganites*	pancakes
τοννοσαλάτα *tonosalata*	tuna salad
τόννος *tonos*	tuna
τυστ κλαμπ *tost 'club'*	toasted club sandwich
τοστ με αυγό/ζαμπόν/τυρί/κοτόπουλο *tost me avgo/zabon/tiri/kotopoolo*	toasted sandwich with egg/ham/cheese/chicken
τοστ με κρέας/μπιφτέκι *tost me kreas/bifteki*	toasted sandwich with meat/hamburger
τούρτα αμυγδάλου *toorta amigthaloo*	almond gateau
τούρτα κρέμα με φράουλες *toorta krema me fraooles*	gateau with strawberries and cream
τούρτα μόκκα *toorta moka*	coffee gateau
τούρτα νουγκατίνα *toorta noogatina*	nougat gateau
τούρτα σαντιγύ *toorta sadiyi*	whipped cream gateau
τούρτα σοκολάτας *toorta sokolatas*	chocolate gateau
τρουφάκια *troofakia*	small chocolate fudge cake
τσάι *tsai*	tea
τσιπούρες ψητές *tsipoores psites*	roast flatfish
τσίπουρο *tsipooro*	kind of ouzo
τσουρέκια *tsoorekia*	sweet bread with fresh butter (Easter time)
τυρί *tiri*	cheese
τυρόπιττα *tiropita*	cheese pie
τυροπιττάκια *tiropitakia*	small cheese pies
φάβα *fava*	continental lentils

MENU GUIDE

φασολάδα *fasolatha*	bean soup
φασολάκια λαδερά *fasolakia lathera*	runner beans in oil
φασολάκια φρέσκα γιαχνί *fasolakia freska yahni*	runner beans with onions and tomato
φασολάκια φρέσκα σαλάτα *fasolakia freska salata*	runner bean salad
φασόλια γίγαντες γιαχνί *fasolia yigades yahni*	butter beans with onion and tomato
φασόλια γίγαντες στο φούρνο *fasolia yigades sto foorno*	oven-cooked butter beans
φέτα *feta*	feta cheese
φιλέ μονιόν *file minion*	thin fillet steak
φιλέτο *fileto*	fillet steak
φοντάν αμυγδάλου *fodan amigthaloo*	almond sweets
φοντάν από καρύδια *fodan apo karithia*	walnut sweets
φοντάν ινδικής καρύδας *fodan inthikis karithas*	coconut sweets
φουντούκι *foodooki*	hazelnut
φράουλες *fraooles*	strawberries
φράουλες με σαντιγύ *fraooles me sadiyi*	strawberries with whipped cream
φρικασέ αρνί *frikase arni*	lamb cooked in lettuce with cream sauce
φρουί-γκλασέ *frooi-glase*	dried assorted fruits with sugar
φρουτοσαλάτα *frootosalata*	fruit salad
φρυγανιές *friganies*	French toast
φύλλο πίττας *filo pitas*	thin pastry
φυστίκια *fistikia*	peanuts
φυστίκια Αιγίνης *fistikia Eyinis*	pistachios
χαβιάρι *haviari*	caviar
χαλβάς *halvas*	halvas, sweet made from sesame seeds and nuts
χάμπουργκερ *'hamburger'*	hamburger
χοιρινό με σέλινο *hirino me selino*	pork casserole with celery
χοιρινό παστό *hirino pasto*	salted pork
χοιρινό σούβλας *hirino soovlas*	pork on the spit

χοιρινό στη σχάρα *hirino sti s-hara*	grilled pork
χοιρινό φούρνου με πατάτες *hirino foornoo me patates*	roast pork with potatoes
χόρτα βρασμένα σαλάτα *horta vrasmena salata*	boiled chicory salad
χορτόσουπα *hortosoopa*	vegetable soup
χταπόδι βραστό *htapothi vrasto*	boiled octopus
χταπόδι κρασάτο *htapothi krasato*	octopus in wine
χταπόδι με μακαρονάκι *htapothi me makaronaki*	octopus with macaroni
χταπόδι πιλάφι *htapothi pilafi*	octopus pilaf
χταπόδι στιφάδο *htapothi stifatho*	octopus with small onions
χυλοπίτες με βούτυρο και τυρί *hilopites me vootiro ke tiri*	tagliatelli with butter and cheese
χυλοπίτες με κοτόπουλο *hilopites me kotopoolo*	tagliatelli with chicken
χυλοπίτες με κιμά *hilopites me kima*	tagliatelli with mince sauce
χυμός *himos*	juice
χυμός ντομάτας *himos domatas*	tomato juice
χωριάτικη σαλάτα *horiatiki salata*	Greek salad – tomatoes, cucumber, feta cheese, peppers and olives
ψάρι βραστό μαγιονέζα *psari vrasto mayoneza*	steamed fish with mayonnaise
ψάρια γλῶσσες βραστές με αυγολέμονο *psaria gloses vrastes me avgolemono*	steamed sole with oil and lemon
ψάρια μαρινάτα *psaria marinata*	marinated fish
ψάρια τηγανητά *psaria tiganita*	fried fish
ψάρια ψητά στη σχάρα *psaria psita sti s-hara*	charcoal-grilled fish
ψαρόσουπα *psarosoopa*	fish soup
ψητός *psitos*	grilled
ψωμί άσπρο/μαύρο *psomi aspro/mavro*	white/brown bread
ψωμί γιά τοστ *psomi ya tost*	sliced bread

SHOPPING

The main thing to remember about shopping in Greece is that most shops will be closed for quite a long period during the middle of the day when the sun is at its hottest. Small village shops will probably be open for 12 hours or more a day, but they are likely to be closed from 1.00 in the afternoon until 4.00. Shops in the towns open from 8.00 am until 2.30 and from 5.00 in the afternoon until 8.30 at night. Shops close on Sundays and public holidays, with the exception of tourist-orientated shops which are usually open all week and at later hours in the evening. The kiosk or 'periptero' (a typical Greek establishment, almost part of the national scene) sells cigarettes, sweets, stamps and postcards as well as a lot of small items that you might need on a day-to-day basis – and it usually has a public telephone as well.

USEFUL WORDS AND PHRASES

Refer to the mini-dictionary for items you may want to ask for.

baker	ο φούρναρης	o foornaris
bookshop	το βιβλιοπωλείο	to vivliopolio
boutique	η μπουτίκ	i bootik
butcher	ο χασάπης	o hasapis
to buy	αγοράζω	agorazo
cake shop	το ζαχαροπλαστείο	to zaharoplastio
cheap	φτηνό	ftino
chemist	το φαρμακείο	to farmakio
fashion	η μόδα	i motha
fishmonger	το ψαράδικο	to psarathiko
florist	το ανθοπωλείο	to anTHopolio
greengrocer	το μανάβικο	to manaviko
grocer	το μπακάλικο	to bakaliko
ironmonger	το σιδεράδικο	to sitherathiko
ladies' wear	τα γυναικεία	ta yinekia

menswear	τα ανδρικά	*ta anthrika*
newsagent	το εφημεριδοπωλείο	*to efimerithopolio*
pharmacy	το φαρμακείο	*to farmakio*
receipt	η απόδειξη	*i apothixi*
record shop	το δισκάδικο	*to thiskathiko*
sales	οι εκπτώσεις	*i ekptosis*
shoe shop	το υποδηματοπωλείο	*to ipothimatopolio*
shop	το μαγαζί	*to magazi*
to go shopping	πάω γιά ψώνια	*pao ya psonia*
souvenir shop	τουριστικά είδη	*tooristika ithi*
special offer	η τιμή ευκαιρίας	*i timi efkerias*
to spend	ξοδεύω	*xothevo*
stationer	το βιβλιοπωλείο	*to vivliopolio*
supermarket	το σούπερ-μάρκετ	*to 'supermarket'*
tailor	ο ράφτης	*o raftis*
till	το ταμείο	*to tamio*
travel agent	το γραφείο ταξειδίων	*to grafio taxithion*
toyshop	το κατάστημα παιχνιδιών	*to katastima pehnithion*

I'd like...
Θα ήθελα…
THа iTHela...

Do you have...?
Εχετε…;
ehete...?

How much is this?
Πόσο κάνει αυτό;
poso kani afto?

Where is the ... department?
Που είναι το τμήμα των…;
poo ine to tmima ton...?

71

Do you have any more of these?
Έχετε κι'αλλα απ'αυτά;
ehete kiala apafta?

I'd like to change this please
Θα ήθελα να το αλλάξω αυτό, παρακαλώ
THa iTHela na to alaxo afto, parakalo

Have you anything cheaper?
Έχετε τίποτα φτηνότερο;
ehete tipota ftinotero?

Have you anything larger?
Έχετε κανένα μεγαλύτερο;
ehete kanena megalitero?

Have you anything smaller?
Έχετε κανένα μικρότερο;
ehete kanena mikrotero?

Does it come in other colours?
Το έχετε σε άλλα χρώματα;
to ehete se ala hromata?

Could you wrap it for me?
Μου το τυλίγετε;
moo to tiliyete?

Can I have a receipt?
Μου δίνετε μία απόδειξη;
moo thinete mia apothixi?

Can I have a bag please?
Μου δίνετε μιά σακούλα, παρακαλώ;
moo thinete mia sakoola, parakalo?

Can I try it (them) on?
Μπορώ να το (τα) δοκιμάσω;
boro na to (ta) thokimaso?

Where do I pay?
Που πληρώνω;
poo plirono?

I'm just looking
Απλώς κυττάω
aplos kitao

I'll come back later
Θα επιστρέψω αργότερα
THa epistrepso argotera

REPLIES YOU MAY BE GIVEN

Exipiretiste?
Are you being served?

Ehete psila?
Have you anything smaller? (= *money*)

Lipame, mas teliose
I'm sorry we're out of stock

Parakalo parte ena karotsaki/kalaTHi
Please take a trolley/basket

Afta ehoome mono
This is all we have

Then epistrefoome hrimata
We cannot give cash refunds

THINGS YOU'LL SEE OR HEAR

αθλητικά *aTHlitika*	sports shop
αλλαντικά *aladika*	salami, sausages, ham, and other meats
ανδρικά *andrika*	men's wear
ανθοπωλείο *anTHopolio*	florist
αντίκες *adikes*	antiques
αρτοποιείο *artopi-io*	bakery
βιβλιοπωλείο *vivliopolio*	book shop
γλυκά *glika*	cakes
γούνες *goones*	furs
γραφείο ταξειδίων *grafio taxithion*	travel agency
γυναικεία *yinekia*	ladies' wear
δεν σιδερώνεται *then sitheronete*	do not iron
δίσκοι-κασσέτες *thiski-kasetes*	records, cassettes
δωδεκάδα *thothekatha*	dozen
είδη γραφείου *ithi grafioo*	office suppliers
είδη εξοχής *ithi exohis*	holiday articles
ειδική προσφορά *ithiki prosfora*	special offer
είσοδος ελευθέρα *isothos elefTHera*	admission free
εκπτώσεις *ekptosis*	sales
ευκαιρία *efkeria*	bargain
εφημερίδες *efimerithes*	newspapers
ζαχαροπλαστείο *zaharoplastio*	cake shop
ηλεκρικά είδη *ilektrika ithi*	electrical goods
ιχθυοπωλείο *ihTHiopolio*	fishmonger
καλλυντικά *kalidika*	perfume and cosmetics
κατεψηγμένα *katepsigmena*	frozen food
καφές *kafes*	coffee
κοσμηματοπωλείο *kosmimatopolio*	jewellery
κρεατοπωλείο *kreatopolio*	butcher
λαχανικά *lahanika*	vegetables
λίρα Αγγλίας *lira Aglias*	pound sterling
μόδα *motha*	fashion

παιδικά *pethika*	children's wear
παιχνίδια *pehnithia*	toys
παντοπωλείο *padopolio*	groceries
περιοδικά *periothika*	magazines
ποιότητα *piotita*	quality
ποτοπωλείο *potopolio*	off-licence, liquor store
ραφείο *rafio*	tailor's
σελφ-σέρβις *'self-service'*	self-service
σιδηρουργείο *sithirooryio*	ironmonger's
τιμή *timi*	price
τμήμα *tmima*	department
το κιλό *to kilo*	a kilo
τσάι *tsai*	tea
υποδήματα *ipothimata*	shoes
φρούτα *froota*	fruit
φτηνό *ftino*	cheap
φωτογραφείο *fotografio*	camera shop
χαλιά *halia*	carpets
ψιλικά *psilika*	small shop

AT THE HAIRDRESSER

There are two types of hairdresser in Greece: the traditional KOYPEIO (barber's) which is only for men and where you can also have a shave, and the KOMMΩTHPIO (hairdresser's) which is for both men and women. They are open on Mondays and Wednesdays from 8 am to 2 pm, and on Tuesdays, Thursdays and Fridays from 8 am to 2 pm and then from 5 pm to 8.30 pm. On Saturdays they open from 8 am to 4 pm.

USEFUL WORDS AND PHRASES

appointment	το ραντεβού	*to radevoo*
beard	τα γένια	*ta yenia*
blond	ξανθιά	*xanTHia*
brush	η βούρτσα	*i voortsa*
comb	η τσατσάρα	*i tsatsara*
conditioner	το κοντίσιονερ	*to 'conditioner'*
curlers	τα μπικουτί	*ta bikooti*
curly	σγουρά	*sgoora*
dark	μαύρα	*mavra*
gel	ο ζελές	*o zeles*
hair	τα μαλλιά	*ta malia*
haircut	το κούρεμα	*to koorema*
hairdresser	η κομμώτρια	*i komotria*
hairdryer	το πιστολάκι	*to pistolaki*
highlights	η μεζ	*i mez*
long	μακριά	*makria*
moustache	το μουστάκι	*to moostaki*
parting	η χωρίστρα	*i horistra*
perm	η περμανάντ	*i permanant*
shampoo	το σαμπουάν	*to sabooan*
shave	το ξύρισμα	*to xirisma*
shaving foam	ο αφρός ξυρίσματος	*o afros xirismatos*
short	κοντά	*koda*

76

styling mousse	η μπριγιαντίνι	*i briyadini*
wavy	κυματιστά	*kimatista*

I'd like to make an appointment
Θα ήθελα να κλείσω ένα ραντεβού
THA iTHela na kliso ena radevoo

Just a trim please
Πάρτε τα μου λίγο, παρακαλώ
parteta moo ligo, parakalo

Not too much off
Μη κόψετε πολλά
mi kopsete pola

A bit more off here please
Λίγο πιό πολύ εδώ, παρακαλώ
ligo pio poli etho, parakalo

I'd like a cut and blow-dry
Θα ήθελα ένα κούρεμα και χτένισμα
THA iTHela ena koorema ke htenisma

I'd like a perm
Θα ήθελα μία περμανάντ
THA iTHela mia permanant

I'd like highlights
Θα ήθελα μία μεζ
THA iTHela mia mez

THINGS YOU'LL SEE OR HEAR

ανδρικαί κομμώσεις	*anthrike komosis*	men's hairdresser
βαφή	*vafi*	hair-dye
βάφω	*vafo*	to tint
ίσια	*isia*	straight
γυναικείαι κομμώσεις	*yineki-e komosis*	ladies' saloon
κόβω	*kovo*	to cut
κομμώσεις	*komosis*	hair stylist
κομμώτρια	*komotria*	hairdresser
κουρέας	*kooreas*	barber
κουρείο	*koorio*	barber (shop)
κούρεμα	*koorema*	haircut
λούσιμο	*loosimo*	wash
μαλλιά	*malia*	hair
μεζ	*mez*	highlights
μιζανπλί	*mizanpli*	set
ξύρισμα	*xirisma*	shave
περμανάντ	*permanant*	perm
ρολά	*rola*	curlers
σαμπουάν	*sambooan*	shampoo
σγουρά	*sgoora*	curly
στεγνώνω	*stegnono*	to dry
τα μπροστινά	*ta brostina*	the front
τα πλαϊνά	*ta plaina*	on the sides
τα πίσω	*ta piso*	at the back

SPORTS

Thanks to Greece's excellent climate almost all outdoor sports are well catered for. Along the coasts of the mainland and on the islands there are excellent opportunities for swimming, water-skiing, sailing, fishing (including underwater fishing) canoeing and sailboarding. You will easily find someone to teach you water-skiing or windsurfing, and hiring equipment generally poses no problem, with everything from a parasol to a sailboard being available at a reasonable charge.

If you want to discover the rarer beauties of Greece and the Archipelago, then you must take to the sea. There are beautiful beaches, small islands and sea caves accessible only by water. And if you don't want to sail solo, there are several companies who will provide you with a captain – and a crew as well if you like. Detailed information is available from the Hellenic Yacht Club, 1 Philellinon Street, Athens.

In the mountainous areas such as the Pinthos range, Parnasos (near Delphi), Parnitha (just north of Athens), or Olympus there is ample scope for walking and mountaineering. In the winter there is also skiing.

USEFUL WORDS AND PHRASES

athletics	ο αθλητισμός	*o aTHlitismos*
ball	η μπάλλα	*i bala*
beach	η παραλία	*i paralia*
bicycle	το ποδήλατο	*to pothilato*
canoe	το κανώ	*to kano*
deckchair	η πολυθρόνα	*i poliTHrona*
diving board	η σανίδα	*i sanitha*
fishing	το ψάρεμα	*to psarema*
fishing rod	το καλάμι	*to kalami*
flippers	τα βατραχοπέδιλα	*ta vatrahopethila*
football	το ποδόσφαιρο	*to pothosfero*

SPORTS

football match	ο ποδοσφαιρικός αγώνας	*o pothosferikos agonas*
goggles	η μάσκα	*i maska*
golf	το γκολφ	*to 'golf'*
golf course	το γήπεδο του γκολφ	*to yipetho too 'golf'*
gymnastics	η γυμναστική	*i yimnastiki*
harpoon	το ψαροντούφεκο	*to psarodoofeko*
jogging	το τζόγκινγκ	*to 'jogging'*
lake	η λίμνη	*i limni*
mountaineering	η ορειβασία	*i orivasia*
oxygen bottles	οι μπουκάλες οξυγόνου	*i bookales oxigonoo*
pedal boat	το ποδήλατο θαλάσσης	*to pothilato THalasis*
racket	η ρακέτα	*i raketa*
riding	η ιππασία	*i ipasia*
rowing boat	η βάρκα με κουπιά	*i varka me koopia*
to run	τρέχω	*treho*
sailboard	το γουίντ-σέρφινγκ	*to 'windsurfing'*
sailing	η ιστιοπλοΐα	*i istioplo-ia*
sand	η άμμος	*i amos*
sea	η θάλασσα	*i THalasa*
skin diving	οι υποβρύχιες καταδύσεις	*i iprovri-hies katathisis*
snorkel	ο αναπνευστήρας	*o anapnefstiras*
stadium	το στάδιο	*to stathio*
sunshade	η ομπρέλα του ήλιου	*i obrela too ilioo*
to swim	κολυμπώ	*kolibo*
swimming pool	η πισίνα	*i pisina*
tennis	το τέννις	*to 'tennis'*
tennis court	το γήπεδο του τέννις	*to yipetho too 'tennis'*
tennis racket	η ρακέτα	*i raketa*
tent	η σκηνή	*i skini*
underwater fishing	το υποβρύχιο ψάρεμα	*to ipovrihio psarema*
volleyball	το βόλλεϋ	*to 'volley'*

walking	το περπάτημα	*to perpatima*
water skiing	το θαλάσσιο σκι	*to THalasio 'ski'*
water skis	τα πέδιλα του σκι	*ta pethila too 'ski'*
wave	το κύμα	*to kima*
wet suit	η στολή	*i stoli*
	βατραχανθρώπου	*vatrahanTHropoo*
yacht	το γιώτ	*to 'yacht'*

How do I get to the beach?
Πως μπορώ να πάω στη παραλία;
pos boro na pao sti paralia?

How deep is the water here?
Πόσο βαθύ είναι το νερό εδώ;
poso vaTHii ine to nero etho?

Is there a swimming pool here?
Υπάρχει καμμία πισίνα εδώ;
iparhi kamia pisina etho?

Is it safe to swim here?
Είναι ασφαλές το κολύμπι εδώ;
ine asfales to kolibi etho?

Can I fish here?
Μπορώ να ψαρέψω εδώ;
boro na psarepso etho?

Do I need a licence?
Χρειάζομαι δίπλωμα;
hriazome thiploma?

How much does it cost per hour/day?
Πόσο στοιχίζει την ώρα/ημέρα;
poso sti-hizi tin ora/imera?

SPORTS

Am I allowed to camp here?
Επιτρέπεται να κατασκηνώσω εδώ;
epitrepete na kataskinoso etho?

I would like to take water-skiing lessons
Θα ήθελα να πάρω μαθήματα σκι
THa iTHela na paro maTHimata 'ski'

Where can I hire...?
Που μπορώ να νοικιάσω...;
poo boro na nikiaso...?

THINGS YOU'LL SEE OR HEAR

αθλητικές εγκαταστάσεις *aTHlitikes egatastasis*	sporting facilities
αθλητικό κέντρο *aTHlitiko* *kedro*	sports centre
ακτή *akti*	beach
άλσος *alsos*	wooded park
απαγορεύεται η κατασκήνωση *apagorevete i kataskinosi*	no camping
απαγορεύεται η κολύμβηση *apagorevete i kolimvisi*	no swimming
απαγορεύεται το ψάρεμα *apagorevete to psarema*	no fishing
απαγορευμένη περιοχή *apagorevmeni periohi*	restricted area
απαγορεύονται οι καταδύσεις *apagorevode i katathisis*	no diving
γήπεδο *yipetho*	football pitch
γήπεδο τέννις *yipetho 'tennis'*	tennis court
εισιτήρια *isitiria*	tickets
ενοικιάζονται *enikiazode*	for hire
θαλάσσια σπορ *THalasia spor*	water sports

ιππόδρομος *ipothromos*	race course (for horses)
ιστιοφόρο *lstioʃoro*	sailing boat
κωπηλατώ *kopīlato*	to row
λιμενική Αστυνομία *limenikį astinomia*	harbour police
λιμήν *limin*	port
μαρίνα *marina*	marina
μαθήματα σκι *maτHimata 'ski'*	water-skiing lessons
πρώτες βοήθειες *protes voiTHies*	first aid
ποδήλατα *pothilata*	bicycles
στάδιο *stathio*	stadium
χώρος διά ποδηλάτες *horos thia pothilates*	cycle path

POST OFFICE

Post offices in Greece only deal with mail, so don't expect to find a telephone there. (If you want to make a phone call, use a call box or go to the telephone exchange – the OTE. Also, if you want to send a telegram, you'll have to go to the OTE and not to a post office.) Stamps can be bought in the post office and also from the kiosk or *periptero,* where you buy your postcards. Letter boxes are yellow in Greece. Mail can be sent to you for collection at the post office of any town – marked poste-restante. Don't forget that you won't be able to collect your mail from the poste-restante unless you have your passport with you.

USEFUL WORDS AND PHRASES

airmail	αεροπορικώς	*aeroporikos*
counter	το ταμείο	*to tamio*
customs form	η τελωνειακή δήλωση	*i teloniaki thilosi*
delivery	η διανομή	*i thianomi*
form	η αίτηση	*i etisi*
letter	το γράμμα	*to grama*
letter box	το γραμματοκιβώτιο	*to gramatokivotio*
mail	το ταχυδρομείο	*to tahithromio*
money order	η ταχυδρομική επιταγή	*i tahithromiki epitayi*
package/parcel	το δέμα	*to thema*
post	το ταχυδρομείο	*to tahithromio*
postage rates	τα ταχυδρομικά έξοδα	*ta tahithromika exotha*
postal order	η ταχυδρομική επιταγή	*i tahithromiki epitayi*
postcard	η κάρτα	*i karta*
postcode	ο ταχυδρομικός τομέας	*o tahithromikos tomeas*

poste-restante	το ποστ-ρεστάντ	*to post-restant*
postman	ο ταχυδρόμος	*o tahithromos*
post office	το ταχυδρομείο	*to tahithromio*
registered letter	το συστημένο γράμμα	*to sistimeno grama*
stamp	το γραμματόσημο	*to gramatosimo*
telegram	το τηλεγράφημα	*to tilegrafima*

How much is a letter/postcard to...?
Πόσο κάνει το γραμματόσημο γιά ένα γράμμα/μία κάρτα γιά...;
poso kani to grumatosimo ya ena grama/mia karta ya...?

I would like three 27 drachma stamps
θα ήθελα τρία γραμματόσημα των είκοσι επτά δραχμών
THa iTHela tria gramatosima ton ikosi epta thrahmon

I want to register this letter
Θέλω να στείλω αυτό το γράμμα συστημένο
THelo na stilo afto to grama sistimeno

I want to send this parcel to...
Θέλω να στείλω αυτό το δέμα στην...
THelo na stilo afto to thema stin...

How long does the post to ... take?
Πόσο κάνει να φτάσει στην...;
poso kani na ftasi stin...?

Where can I post this?
Που μπορώ να ταχυδρομήσω αυτό;
poo boro na tahithromiso afto?

Is there any mail for me?
Υπάρχει κανένα γράμμα γιά μένα
iparhi kanena grama ya mena?

85

POST OFFICE

I'd like to send a telegram
Θα ήθελα να στείλω ένα τηλεγράφημα
THA iTHela na stilo ena tilegrafima

This is to go airmail
Αυτό να πάει αεροπορικώς
afto na pai aeroporikos

THINGS YOU'LL SEE OR HEAR

αεροπορικώς *aeroporikos*	by air mail
ανοικτά *anikta*	open
αποστολέας *apostoleas*	sender
γραμματοκιβώτιο *gramatokivotio*	letter box
γραμματόσημα *gramatosima*	stamps
δέματα *themata*	parcels, packages
διεύθυνση *thi-efthinsi*	address
ΕΛΤΑ *ELTA*	Greek Post Office
εξωτερικού *exoterikoo*	postage abroad
επιστολές *epistoles*	letters
εσωτερικού *esoterikoo*	inland postage
καρτ-ποστάλ *kart-postal*	postcard
κατεπείγον *katepigon*	express
κλειστά *klista*	closed
ποστ-ρεστάντ *post-restant*	poste-restante
συστημένα *sistimena*	registered mail
ταχυδρομείο *tahithromio*	post office
ταχυδρομικός τομεύς *tahithromikos tomefs*	post code
τηλεγραφήμματα *tilegrafimata*	telegrams
ώρες λειτουργίας *ores litooryias*	opening hours

TELEPHONE

Telephones and telegrams are the responsibility of the OTE (Telecommunications Organization of Greece), not of the post office. The public phone boxes are blue for local calls and orange for long distance.

Don't forget that the little Greek kiosks where you can buy cigarettes, postcards etc, also have a telephone for public use. There are pay-phones in cafeterias and restaurants, but if you want to make a call home (or a long distance call within Greece) it is best to go to an OTE. There you will be given a booth and asked to pay at the desk when you have finished your call.

On Greek phones you will hear the same dialling tone as in the UK or the USA; a repeated long tone means that the number is ringing, while rapid pips indicate an engaged number. Dialling codes: UK – 0044, USA – 001.

Some useful telephone numbers are:

Medical care	166
Police	100
Tourist Police	171
Fire	199
Roadside assistance	104

USEFUL WORDS AND PHRASES

call	το τηλεφώνημα	to tilefonima
to call	τηλεφωνώ	tilefono
code	ο κωδικός	o kothikos
crossed line	η μπλεγμένη γραμμή	i blegmeni grami
to dial	καλώ	kalo
emergency	η επείγουσα ανάγκη	i epigoosa anagi
enquiries	οι πληροφορίες	i plirofories

87

extension	το εσωτερικό	*to esoteriko*
international call	το υπεραστικό	*to iperastiko*
number	ο αριθμός	*o arithmos*
pay-phone	το τηλέφωνο με κέρματα	*to tilefono me kermata*
receiver	το ακουστικό	*to akoostiko*
reverse charge call	το τηλεφώνημα κολέκτ	*to tilefonima kolekt*
telephone	το τηλέφωνο	*to tilefono*
telephone box	ο τηλεφωνικός θάλαμος	*o tilefonikos THalamos*
telephone directory	ο τηλεφωνικός κατάλογος	*o tilefonikos katalogos*
wrong number	λάθος νούμερο	*laTHos noomero*

Where is the nearest phone box?
Που είναι ο πλησιέστερος τηλεφωνικός θάλαμος;
poo ine o plisi-esteros tilefonikos THalamos?

Hello, this is ... speaking
Χαίρετε, είμαι ο…
herete, ime o...

Is that...?
Ο/η…;
o/i...?

Speaking
Ο ίδιος
o ithios

I would like to speak to...
Θα ήθελα να μιλήσω στον…
THa iTHela na miliso ston...

Extension ... please
Εσωτερικό ... παρακαλώ
esoteriko ... parakalo

Please tell him ... called
Παρακαλώ του λέτε ότι τηλεφώνησε ο...
parakalo tou lete oti tilefonise o...

Ask him to call me back please
Πέστε του να με ξαναπάρει παρακαλώ
peste too na me xanapari parakalo

My number is...
Το τηλέφωνό μου είναι...
to tilefono moo ine...

Do you know where he is?
Ξέρετε που είναι;
xerete poo ine?

When will he be back?
Πότε θα επιστρέψει;
pote THA epistrepsi?

Could you leave him a message?
Μπορείτε να του αφήσετε ένα μήνυμα;
borite na too afisete ena minima?

I'll ring back later
Θα σε ξαναπάρω αργότερα
THA se xanaparo argotera

Sorry, wrong number
Πήρατε λάθος αριθμό
pirate laTHos ariTHmo

REPLIES YOU MAY BE GIVEN

O ithios
Speaking

Lipame, then ine etho
Sorry, he's not in

Pios tilefoni?
Who's calling?

Me pion THelete na milisete?
Who would you like to speak to?

Bori na sas pari piso?
Can he call you back?

Pio ine to tilefono sas?
What's your number?

Pirate laTHos noomero
You've got the wrong number

THa epistrepsi stis...
He'll be back at...

THa sas sintheso
I'll put you through

Is there a telephone directory?
Υπάρχει κανένας τηλεφωνικός κατάλογος;
iparhi kanenas tilefonikos katalogos?

I would like the directory for...
Θα ήθελα τον κατάλογο γιά…
THa iTHela ton katalogo ya...

Can I call abroad from here?
Μπορώ να τηλεφωνήσω στο εξωτερικό από εδώ;
boro na tilefoniso sto exoteriko apo etho?

How much is a call to...?
Πόσο στοιχίζει ένα τηλεφώνημα στο…;
poso sti-hizi ena tilefonima sto...?

I would like to reverse the charges
Θα ήθελα τα έξοδα να πληρωθούν εκεί
THa iTHela ta exotha na pliroTIIoon eki

I would like a number in...
Θέλω ένα αριθμό στην…
THelo ena ariTHmo stin...

THINGS YOU'LL SEE OR HEAR

ακουστικό	*akoostiko*	receiver
άμεσος δράσις	*amesos thrasis*	emergencies, police
αριθμός	*ariTHmos*	number
δεν λειτουργεί	*then litooryi*	out of order
καλεί	*kali*	it's ringing
κέρματα	*kermata*	coins
κωδικός	*kothikos*	code
λάθος νούμερο	*laTHos noomero*	wrong number
μιλάει	*milai*	engaged
μονάδες	*monathes*	units
καλέσατε	*kalesate*	dial
νούμερο	*noomero*	number
ΟΤΕ	*Ote*	telephone
πυροσβεστική	*pirosvestiki*	fire brigade
σηκώσατε	*sikosate*	pick up
τηλεγραφήματα	*tilegrafimata*	telegrams
τηλεφώνημα	*tilefonima*	call
τηλεφωνικός θάλαμος	*tilefonikos THalamos*	telephone box
τηλεφωνικός κατάλογος *tilefonikos katalogos*		telephone directory
τηλέφωνο	*tilefono*	telephone
τηλεφωνώ	*tilefono*	to call
τοπικό	*topiko*	local call
φωτιά	*fotia*	fire
χαίρετε	*herete*	hello
χρυσός οδηγός	*hrisos othigos*	yellow pages
υπεραστικό	*iperastiko*	long distance call, international call

HEALTH

Under the EEC Social Security regulations visitors from the UK qualify for treatment on the same basis as the Greeks themselves. You must complete the form CM1 (at your own Social Security office) a month at least before travelling. You then get a certificate (E111) for use if you need treatment, plus an explanatory leaflet.

If you fall ill or have an accident – nothing too serious – you can always go to a chemist, who is usually qualified to treat minor injuries. Chemists' (pharmacies, *to farmakio*) are identified by a red cross, and all towns have one that is open all night on a rota system; look for a sign on the door telling you which is the duty chemist.

USEFUL WORDS AND PHRASES

accident	το ατύχημα	*to atihima*
ambulance	το ασθενοφόρο	*to asTHenoforo*
anaemic	αναιμικός	*anemikos*
appendicitis	η σκωληκοειδίτις	*i skoliko-ithitis*
appendix	η σκωληκοειδής απόφυση	*i skoliko-ithis apofisi*
aspirin	η ασπιρίνη	*i aspirini*
asthma	το άσθμα	*to asTHma*
backache	ο πόνος στη πλάτη	*o ponos sti plati*
bandage	ο επίδεσμος	*o epithesmos*
bite	το δάγκωμα	*to thagoma*
(of insect)	το τσίμπημα	*to tsibima*
bladder	η κύστη	*i kisti*
blister	η φουσκάλα	*i fooskala*
blood	το αίμα	*to ema*
blood donor	ο αιμοδότης	*o emothotis*
burn	το κάψιμο	*o kapsimo*
cancer	ο καρκίνος	*o karkinos*
chemist	ο φαρμακοποιός	*o farmakopios*
chest	το στήθος	*to stiTHos*

chickenpox	η ανεμοβλογιά	*i anemovloya*
cold	το κρυολόγημα	*to krioloyima*
concussion	η διάσειση	*i thiasisi*
constipation	η δυσκοιλιότητα	*i thiskiliotita*
contact lenses	οι φακοί επαφής	*i faki epafis*
corn	ο κάλος	*o kalos*
cough	ο βήχας	*o vihas*
cut	το κόψιμο	*to kopsimo*
dentist	ο οδοντίατρος	*o othodiatros*
diabetes	το ζάχαρο	*to zaharo*
diarrhoea	η διάρροια	*i thiaria*
dizzy	ζαλισμένος	*zalismenos*
doctor	ο γιατρός	*o yatros*
earache	ο πόνος στ'αυτί	*o ponos st'afti*
fever	ο πυρετός	*o piretos*
filling	το σφράγισμα	*to sfrayisma*
first aid	οι πρώτες βοήθειες	*i protes voiTHies*
flu	η γρίππη	*i gripi*
fracture	το κάταγμα	*to katagma*
German measles	η ερυθρά	*i eriTHra*
glasses	τα γυαλιά	*ta yalia*
haemorrhage	η αιμοραγία	*i emorayia*
hayfever	ο πυρετός εκ χόρτου	*o piretos ek hortoo*
headache	ο πονοκέφαλος	*o ponokefalos*
heart	η καρδιά	*i karthia*
heart attack	η καρδιακή προσβολή	*i karthiaki prosvoli*
hospital	το νοσοκομείο	*to nosokomio*
ill	άρρωστος	*arostos*
indigestion	η δυσπεψία	*i thispepsia*
injection	η ένεση	*i enesi*
itch	η φαγούρα	*i fagoora*
kidney	το νεφρό	*to nefro*
lump	ο όγκος	*o ogos*
measles	η ιλαρά	*i ilara*
migraine	η ημικρανία	*i imikrania*
mumps	οι μαγουλάδες	*i magoolathes*

nausea	η ναυτία	*i naftia*
nurse	η νοσοκόμα	*i nosokoma*
operation	η εγχείρηση	*i enhirisi*
optician	ο οπτικός	*o optikos*
pain	ο πόνος	*o ponos*
penicillin	η πενικιλλίνη	*i penikilini*
plaster	ο γύψος	*o yipsos*
pneumonia	η πνευμονία	*i pnevmonia*
pregnant	έγκυος	*egios*
prescription	η συνταγή	*i sidayi*
rheumatism	οι ρευματισμοί	*i revmatismi*
scald	το έγκαυμα	*to egavma*
scratch	η γρατζουνιά	*i grazoonia*
smallpox	η ευλογιά	*i evloya*
splinter	η αγκίδα	*i agitha*
sprain	το διάστρεμμα	*to thiastrema*
sting	το τσούξιμο	*to tsooximo*
stomach	το στομάχι	*to stomahi*
temperature	ο πυρετός	*o piretos*
tonsils	οι αμυγδαλές	*i amigthales*
toothache	ο πονόδοντος	*o ponothodos*
travel sickness	η ναυτία	*i naftia*
ulcer	το έλκος	*to elkos*
vaccination	ο εμβολιασμός	*o emvoliasmos*
to vomit	κάνω εμετό	*kano emeto*
whooping cough	ο κοκκύτης	*o kokitis*

I have a pain in...
Έχω ένα πόνο στο...
eho ena pono sto...

I do not feel well
Δεν αισθάνομαι καλά
then esthanome kala

HEALTH

I feel faint
Μου έρχεται λιποθυμία
moo erhete lipoτΗimia

I'm feeling sick
Θα κάνω εμετό
ΤΗa kano emeto

I feel dizzy
Ζαλίζομαι
zalizome

I have a sore throat
Πονάει ο λαιμός μου
ponai o lemos moo

It hurts here
Πονάει εδώ
ponai etho

It's a sharp pain
Είναι δυνατός ο πόνος
ine thinatos o ponos

It's a dull pain
Έχω ένα μικρό πόνο
eho ena mikro pono

It hurts all the time
Πονάει συνέχεια
ponai sinehia

It only hurts now and then
Με πονάει πότε-πότε
me ponai pote-pote

It hurts when you touch it
Με πονάει όταν το ακουμπάς
me ponai otan to akoobas

It hurts more at night
Πονάει περισσότερο τη νύχτα
ponai perisotero ti nihta

It stings
Τσούζει
tsoozi

It aches
Πονάει
ponai

I have a temperature
Έχω πυρετό
eho pireto

I need a prescription for...
Χρειάζομαι συνταγή γιά...
hriazome sidayi ya...

I normally take...
Συνήθως παίρνω...
siniTHos perno

I'm allergic to...
Είμαι αλλεργικός με...
ime aleryikos me...

Have you got anything for...?
Εχετε τίποτα γιά...;
ehete tipota ya...?

97

HEALTH

Do I need a prescription for...?
χρειάζομαι συνταγή γιά...;
hriazome sidayi ya...?

I have lost a filling
Μου έφυγε ένα σφράγισμα
moo efiye ena sfrayisma

REPLIES YOU MAY BE GIVEN

Na pernis ... hapia/thiskia tin imera
Take ... pills/tablets per day

Me nero
With water

Na ta masate
Chew them

Mia fora/thio fores/tris fores tin imera
Once/twice/three times a day

Mono otan pas ya ipno
Only when you go to bed

Ti pernis siniTHos?
What do you normally take?

Prepi na this ena yatro
I think you should see a doctor

Lipame, then to ehoome
I'm sorry, we don't have that

Hriazese sidayi yafto
For that you need a prescription

THINGS YOU'LL SEE OR HEAR

αίθουσα αναμονής *eTHoosa anamonis*	waiting room
ακτίνες-X *aktines hi*	X-rays
ασθενοφόρο *asTHenoforo*	ambulance
γιατρός *yatros*	doctor
γυαλιά *yalia*	glasses
γυναικολόγος *yinekologos*	gynaecologist
δερματολόγος-αφροδισιολόγος *thermatologos-afrothisiologos*	dermatologist, venereal specialist
διανυκτερεύον *thianikterevon*	open all night
ειδικός *ithikos*	specialist
εξετάσεις *exetasis*	check-up
ησυχία *isihia*	quiet
ιατρείο *iatrio*	doctor's surgery
ιατρός *iatros*	doctor
κλινική *kliniki*	clinic
νοσοκόμα *nosokoma*	nurse
νοσοκομείο *nosokomio*	hospital
οδοντιατρός *othodiatros*	dentist
οδοντογιατρείο *othodoyatrio*	dentist's
ούλο *oolo*	gum
οπτικός *optikos*	optician
παθολόγος *paTHologos*	GP
παιδίατρος *pethiatros*	paediatrician
πίεση αίματος *pi-esi ematos*	blood pressure
πρώτες βοήθειες *protes voiTHi-es*	first aid
αφράγισμα *sfrayisma*	filling
τοπική αναισθησία *topiki anesTHisia*	local anesthestic
φαρμακείο *farmakio*	chemist (shop)
φαρμακοποιός *farmakopios*	chemist
χειρουργείο *hirooryio*	operating theatre
ώρες επισκέψεως *ores episkepseos*	visiting hours

CONVERSION TABLES

DISTANCES

Distances are marked in kilometres. To convert kilometres to miles, divide the km. by 8 and multiply by 5 (one km. being five-eighths of a mile). Convert miles to km. by dividing the miles by 5 and multiplying by 8. A mile is 1609m. (1.609km.).

km.	miles or km.	miles
1.61	**1**	0.62
3.22	**2**	1.24
4.83	**3**	1.86
6.44	**4**	2.48
8.05	**5**	3.11
9.66	**6**	3.73
11.27	**7**	4.35
12.88	**8**	4.97
14.49	**9**	5.59
16.10	**10**	6.21

Other units of length:

1 centimetre = 0.39 in.	1 inch = 25.4 millimetres
1 metre = 39.37 in.	1 foot = 0.30 metre (30 cm.)
10 metres = 32.81 ft.	1 yard = 0.91 metre

WEIGHTS

The unit you will come into most contact with is the kilogram (kilo), equivalent to 2 lb 3 oz. To convert kg. to lbs., multiply by 2 and add one-tenth of the result (thus, 6 kg x 2 = 12 + 1.2, or 13.2 lbs). One ounce is about 28 grams, and 1 lb is 454 g.

grams	ounces		ounces	grams
50	1.76		1	28.3
100	3.53		2	56.7
250	8.81		4	113.4
500	17.63		8	226.8

kg.	lbs. *or* kg.	lbs.
0.45	1	2.20
0.91	2	4.41
1.36	3	6.61
1.81	4	8.82
2.27	5	11.02
2.72	6	13.23
3.17	7	15.43
3.63	8	17.64
4.08	9	19.84
4.53	10	22.04

TEMPERATURE

To convert centigrade or Celsius degrees into Fahrenheit, the accurate method is to multiply the °C figure by 1.8 and add 32. Similarly, to convert °F to °C, subtract 32 from the °F figure and divide by 1.8. This will give you a truly accurate conversion, but takes a little time in mental arithmetic! See the table below.

°C	°F		°C	°F	
-10	14		25	77	
0	32		30	86	
5	41		36.9	98.4	body temperature
10	50		40	104	
20	68		100	212	boiling point

CONVERSION TABLES

LIQUIDS

Motorists from the UK will be used to seeing petrol priced per litre (and may even know that one litre is about $1\frac{1}{4}$ pints). One 'imperial' gallon is roughly $4\frac{1}{2}$ litres, but USA drivers must remember that the American gallon is only 3.8 litres (1 litre = 1.06 US quart). In the following table, imperial gallons are used:

litres	gals. or l.	gals.
4.54	1	0.22
9.10	2	0.44
13.64	3	0.66
18.18	4	0.88
22.73	5	1.10
27.27	6	1.32
31.82	7	1.54
36.37	8	1.76
40.91	9	1.98
45.46	10	2.20
90.92	20	4.40
136.38	30	6.60
181.84	40	8.80
227.30	50	11.00

TYRE PRESSURES

lb/sq.in.	15	18	20	22	24
kg/sq.cm.	1.1	1.3	1.4	1.5	1.7

lb/sq.in.	26	28	30	33	35
kg/sq.cm.	1.8	2.0	2.1	2.3	2.5

MINI—DICTIONARY

about: about 16 peripoo thekaexi
accelerator to gazi
accident to thistihima
accommodation thomatia
ache o ponos
adaptor *(electrical)* to polaplo
address i thiefthinsi
adhesive i kola
after meta
after-shave i kolonia meta to xirisma
again xana
against enadion
air-conditioning o klimatismos
aircraft to aeroplano
air freshener to aposmitiko horoo
air hostess i aerosinothos
airline i aerogrami
airport to aerothromio
Albania i Alvania
Albanian *(man)* o Alvanos
 (woman) i Alvani
 (adj) Alvanikos
alcohol to alko-ol
all ola
 all the streets oli i thromi
 that's all, thanks tipota alo, efharisto
almost s-hethon
alone monos
already ithi
always pada
am: I am ime
ambulance to asthenoforo
America i Ameriki

American *(man)* o Amerikanos
 (woman) i Amerikana
 (adj) Amerikanikos
and ke
ankle o astragalos
anorak to boofan
another *(room)* alo
 (coffee) kialo
anti-freeze to adipsiktiko
antique shop to paleopolio
antiseptic to adisiptiko
apartment to thiamerisma
aperitif to aperitif
appendicitis i skolikoithitis
appetite i orexi
apple to milo
application form i etisi
appointment to radevoo
apricot to verikoko
are: you are ise
 we are imaste
 they are ine
arm to heri
art i tehni
art gallery i pinakothiki
artist o kalitehnis
as: as soon as possible oso pio grigora yinete
ashtray to stahtothohio
asleep: he's asleep kimate
aspirin i aspirini
at: at the post office sto tahithromio
 at night ti nihta
 at 3 o'clock stis tris i ora

Athens i ATHina
attractive elkistikos
aunt i thia
Australia i Afstralia
Australian *(man)* o Afstralos
  (woman) i Afstraleza
  (adj) Afstralezikos
Austria i Afstria
Austrian *(man)* Afstriakos
  (woman) i Afstriaki
  (adj) Afstriakos
automatic aftomatos
away: is it far away? ine makria?
  go away! fiye!
awful apesios
axe to tsekoori
axle o axonas

baby to moro
back *(not front)* piso
  (body) i plati
bacon to 'bacon'
  bacon and eggs avga me 'bacon'
bad kakos
bait to tholoma
bake psino
baker o foornaris
balcony to balkoni
ball *(football)* i bala
  (tennis) to balaki
  (dance) i horoesperitha
ball-point pen o markathoros
banana i banana
band *(musicians)* to sigrotima
bandage o epithesmos
bank i trapeza
banknote to hartonomisma

bar to bar
  bar of chocolate i sokolata
barbecue to psisimo stin exohi
barber's to koorio
bargain i efkeria
basement to ipoyio
basin *(sink)* o niptiras
basket to kalaTHi
bath to banio
  to have a bath kano banio
bathing hat o skoofos too banioo
bathroom to banio
battery i bataria
beach i paralia
beans ta fasolia
beard ta yenia
because epithi
bed to krevati
bed linen ta sedonia
bedroom to ipnothomatio
beef to mos-hari
beer i bira
before prin
beginner o arharios
behind apo piso
beige bez
Belgian *(man)* o Velgos
  (woman) i Velyitha
  (adj) Velyikos
Belgium to Velyio
bell *(church)* i kabana
  (door) to koothooni
below apo kato
belt i zoni
beside thipla apo
best aristos
better kaliteros

between metaxi

bicycle to pothilato

big megalos

bikini to bikini

bill o logariasmos

bin liner i sakoola skoopithion

bird to pooli

birthday ta yeneTHlia
  happy birthday! hronia pola!

birthday present to thoro ton
  yeneTHlion

biscuit to biskoto

bite *(verb)* thagono
  (noun) i thagonia
  (by insect) to tsibima

bitter pikros

black mavros

blackberry to mooro

blanket i kooverta

bleach *(verb: hair)* xasprizo
  (noun) i hlorini

blind *(cannot see)* o tiflos

blister i fooskala

blood to ema

blouse i blooza

blue ble

boat to plio
  (smaller) to kaiki

body to soma

boil vrazo

bolt *(verb)* sirtono
  (noun: on door) o sirtis

bone to kokalo

bonnet *(car)* to kapo

book *(noun)* to vivlio
  (verb) klino

booking office to praktorio

isitirion

bookshop to vivliopolio

boot *(car)* to port-bagaz
  (footwear) i bota

border ta sinora

boring varetos

born: I was born in... *(date)*
  yeniTHika to...

both ke i thio

both of them i thio toos
  both of us i thio mas
  both ... and... ke ... ke...

bottle to bookali

bottle-opener to anihtiri

bottom o patos
  (sea) o viTHos

bowl to bol

box to kooti

boy to agori

boyfriend o filos

bra to soutien

bracelet to vrahioli

braces i tirades

brake *(noun)* to freno
  (verb) frenaro

brandy to koniak

bread to psomi

breakdown *(car)* i mihaniki vlavi
  (nervous) o nevrikos klonismos

breakfast to proino

breathe anapneo
  I can't breathe then boro na
  anapnefso

bridge i yefira

briefcase o hartofilakas

British Vretanikos

brochure to thiafimistiko

broken spasmeno
   broken leg to spasmeno pothi
brooch i karfitsa
brother o athelfos
brown kafes
bruise i melania
brush *(noun)* i voortsa
   (paint) to pinelo
   (verb) voortsizo
bucket o koovas
building to ktirio
Bulgaria i Voolgaria
Bulgarian *(man)* o Voolgaros
   (woman) i Voolgara
   (adj) Voolgarikos
bumper o profilahtiras
burglar o thiariktis
burn *(verb)* keo
   (noun) to kapsimo
bus to leoforio
business i thoolies
   it's none of your business then
   se afora
bus station o staτμos leoforion
busy *(occupied)* katilimenos
   (bar) polisihnastos
but ala
butcher o hasapis
butter to vootiro
button to koobi
buy agorazo
by: by the window koda sto
   paraτμiro
   by Friday eos tin paraskevi
   by myself monos moo

cabbage to lahano

cable car to teleferik
cafe i kafeteria
cagoule o aτμiavroho
cake to 'cake'
cake shop to zaharoplastio
calculator to kobiooteraki
call: what's it called?
   pos to lene?
camera i fotografiki mihani
campsite to 'camping'
camshaft o strofalos
can *(tin)* konserva
   can I have...? boro na eho...?
Canada o Kanathas
Canadian *(man)* o Kanathos
   (woman) i Kanatheza
   (adj) Kanathezikos
cancer o karkinos
candle to keri
canoe to kano
cap *(bottle)* to kapaki
   (hat) o skoofos
car to aftokinito
caravan to trohospito
carburettor to karbirater
card i karta
cardigan i zaketa
careful prosektikos
   be careful! prosehe!
carpet to hali
carriage *(train)* to vagoni
carrot to karoto
carry-cot to port-bebe
case i valitsa
cash ta metrita
   (coins) ta psila
   to pay cash plirono metritis

cassette i kaseta
cassette player to kasetofono
castle to kastro
cat i gata
cathedral o kaTHethrikos naos
cauliflower to koonoopithi
cave i spilia
cemetery to nekrotafio
centre to kedro
certificate to pistopi-itiko
chair i karekla
chambermaid i kamariera
chamber music i moosiki
   thomatioo
change *(noun: money)* ta resta
   (verb: clothes) alazo
cheap ftinos
cheers! is iyian!
cheese to tiri
chemist *(shop)* to farmakio
cheque i epitayi
cheque book to karne ton
   epitagon
cherry to kerasi
chess to skaki
chest to stiTHos
chewing gum i tsihla
chicken to kotopoolo
child to pethi
children ta pethia
china i porselani
China i Kina
Chinese *(man)* o Kinezos
   (woman) i Kineza
   (adj) Kinezikos
chips i tiganites patates
chocolate i sokolata

box of chocolates to kooti
me ta sokolatakia
chop *(food)* i brizola
   (to cut) kovo
Christian name to mikro onoma
church i eklisia
cigar to pooro
cigarette to tsigaro
cinema o kinimatografos
city i poli
city centre to kedro tis polis
class i THesi
classical music i klasiki moosiki
clean kaTHaros
clear *(obvious)* faneros
   (water) thiavyes
   is that clear? to katalaves?
clever exipnos
clock to roloi
   (alarm) to xipnitiri
close *(near)* koda
   (stuffy) apopniktikos
   (verb) klino
   the shop is closed to magazi
   eklise
clothes ta rooha
club to 'club'
   (cards) to bastooni
clutch to debrayaz
coach to poolman
   (of train) to vagoni
coach station o staTHmos
   iperastikon leoforion
coat to palto
coathanger i kremastra
cockroach i katsaritha
coffee o kafes

coin to kerma
cold *(illness)* to krioma
 (adj) krios
collar to kolaro
collection *(stamps etc)*
 i siloyi
colour to hroma
colour film to enhromo 'film'
comb *(noun)* i tsatsara
 (verb) htenizome
come erhome
 I come from... ime apo...
 we came last week irthame tin
 perasmeni evthomatha
 come here! ela!
communication cord to
 koothooni kinthinoo
compartment to vagoni
complicated poliplokos
concert i sinavlia
conditioner *(hair)* to 'conditioner'
conductor *(bus)* o ispraktoras
 (orchestra) o maestros
congratulations! sinharitiria!
constipation i thiskiliotis
consulate to proxenio
contact lenses i faki epafis
contraceptive to profilaktiko
cook *(noun)* o mayiras
 (verb) mayirevo
cooking utensils ta mayirika skevi
cool throseros
Corfu i Kerkira
cork o felos
corkscrew to anihtiri
corner i gonia
corridor o thiathromos

cosmetics ta kalidika
cost *(verb)* stihizo
 what does it cost? poso kani
 afto?
cotton to vamvakero
cotton wool to vamvaki
cough *(verb)* viho
 (noun) o vihas
country *(state)* i hora
 (not town) i exohi
cousin *(male)* o exathelfos
 (female) i exathelfi
crab to kavoori
cramp i kramba
crayfish i karavitha
cream i krema
credit card i pistotiki karta
Crete i Kriti
crew to pliroma
crisps ta tsips
crowded yemato kosmo
cruise i krooaziera
crutches i pateritses
cry *(weep)* kleo
 (shout) fonazo
cucumber to agoori
cufflinks ta maniketokooba
cup to flitzani
cupboard to doolapi
curlers ta bikooti
curls i bookles
curry metafero
curtain i koortina
Customs to telonio
cut *(noun)* to kopsimo
 (verb) kovo

dad o babas
dairy *(shop)* to galaktopolio
damp igros
dance o horos
dangerous epikinthinos
dark skotinos
daughter i kori
day i imera
dead nekros
deaf koofos
dear *(person)* agapitos
 (expensive) akrivos
deckchair i politHrona
deep vaTHis
deliberately epitithes
dentist o othodiatros
dentures i masela
deny arnoome
 I deny it to arnoome
deodorant to aposmitiko
department store to katastima
departure i anahorisi
develop *(a film)* emfanizo
diamond *(jewel)* to thiamadi
 (cards) to karo
diarrhoea i thiaria
diary to imeroloyio
dictionary to lexiko
die peTHeno
diesel to 'diesel'
different thiaforetikos
 that's different afto ine alo
 I'd like a different one THelo
 ena alo
difficult thiskolos
dining car to estiatorio too trenoo
dining room i trapezaria

directory *(telephone)* o
 tilefonikos katalogos
dirty vromikos
disabled anapiros
distributor *(car)* to distribiooter
dive vooto
diving board i sanitha
divorced horismenos
do kano
doctor o yatros
document to engrafo
dog o skilos
doll i kookla
dollar to tholario
door i porta
double room to thiplo thomatio
doughnut to donat
down kato
drawing pin i pineza
dress to forema
drink *(verb)* pino
 (noun) to poto
 would you like a drink?
 THelis ena poto?
drinking water to posimo nero
drive *(verb)* othigo
driver o othigos
driving licence to thiploma
 othiyiseos
drunk meTHismenos
dry stegnos
dry cleaner to stegnokaTHaristirio
dummy *(for baby)* i pipila
during kata ti thiarkia
dustbin o skoopithodenekes
duster to xeskonopano
Dutch Olanthikos

109

duty-free aforoloyita

each *(every)* katHenas
  twenty drachma each ikosi
  thrahmes to katHena
early noris
earrings ta skoolarikia
ears ta aftia
east i anatoli
easy efkolos
egg to avgo
either: either of them
  opio nane
  either ... or... i ... i...
elastic elastikos
elastic band to lastihaki
elbow o agonas
electric ilektrikos
electricity to ilektriko
else: something else kati alo
  someone else kapios alos
  somewhere else kapoo aloo
embarrassing dropiastikos
embassy i presvia
embroidery to kedima
emerald to smaragthi
emergency i epigoosa anagi
empty athios
end to telos
engaged *(couple)* aravoniasmenos
  (occupied) katilimenos
engine *(motor)* i mihani
England i Aglia
English Aglikos
  (language) ta Aglika
Englishman o Aglikos

Englishwoman i Aglitha
enlargement i meyentHisi
enough arketa
entertainment i thiaskethasi
entrance i isothos
envelope o fakelos
escalator i kinites skales
especially ithi-etera
evening to vrathi
every katHe
everyone oli
everything katHe ti
everywhere opoothipote
example to parathigma
  for example parathigmatos hari
excellent iperohos
excess baggage to ipervaro
exchange *(verb)* adalaso
exchange rate i timi sinalagmatos
excursion i ekthromi
excuse me! signomi!
exit i exothos
expensive akrivos
extension lead i proektasi
eye drops i stagones ya ta
  matia
eyes ta matia

face to prosopo
faint *(unclear)* asafis
  (verb) lipotHimo
  to feel faint estHanome
  lipotHimia
fair *(funfair)* to paniyiri
  it's not fair then ine thikeo
false teeth ta pseftika thodia

family i ikoyenia
fan *(ventilator)* o anemistiras
  (enthusiast) o тнаvmastis
fan belt to loori too ventilater
far makria
  how far is...? poso makria
  ine...?
fare i timi too isitirioo
farm to agroktima
farmer o agrotis
fashion i motha
fast grigoros
fat *(of person)* to pahos
  (on meat etc) to lipos
father o pateras
feel *(touch)* agizo
  I feel hot zestenome
  I feel like... eho epiтнimia
  ya...
  I don't feel well then
  estнanome kala
feet ta pothia
felt-tip pen o markathoros
ferry to feri-bot
fever o piretos
fiancé o aravoniastikos
fiancée i aravoniastikia
field to horafi
fig to siko
filling *(tooth)* to sfrayisma
  (sandwich etc) i yemisi
film to 'film'
filter to filtro
finger to thaktilo
fire i fotia
  (blaze) i pirkaya
fire extinguisher o pirosvestiras

firework to pirotehnima
first protos
first aid i protes voiтнies
first floor to proto patoma
fish to psari
fishing to psarema
  to go fishing pao ya psarema
fishing rod to psarokalamo
fishmonger o psaras
fizzy me anтнrakiko
flag i simea
flash *(camera)* to flas
flat *(level)* epipethos
  (apartment) to thiamerisma
flavour i yefsi
flea o psilos
flight i ptisi
flip-flops i sayionares
flippers ta vatrahopethila
flour to alevri
flower to looloothi
flu i gripi
flute to flaooto
fly *(verb)* peto
  (insect) i miga
fog i omihli
folk music i thimotiki moosiki
food to fai
food poisoning i trofiki
  thilitiriasi
football to pothosfero
  (ball) i bala
for ya
  for me ya mena
  what for? ya pio logo
  for a week ya mia evthomatha
foreigner o xenos

forest to thasos
fork to pirooni
fortnight to thekapanTHimero
fountain pen i pena
fourth tetartos
fracture to katagma
France i Galia
free eleftheros
  (no cost) thore-an
freezer i katapsixi
French Galikos
Frenchman o Galos
Frenchwoman i Galitha
fridge to psiyio
friend o filos
friendly filikos
front: in front of... brosta apo...
frost i pagonia
fruit to frooto
fruit juice o himos frooton
fry tiganizo
frying pan to tigani
full yematos
  I'm full hortasa
full board fool pansion
funnel (for pouring) to honi
funny astios
  (odd) peri-ergos
furniture to epipla

garage to garaz
garden o kipos
garlic to skortho
gas-permeable lenses
  i imiskliri faki epafis
gay (happy) haroomenos

  (homosexual) o omofilofilos
gear i tahitita
gear lever o mohlos tahititon
gents (toilet) i tooaleta anthron
German (man) o Yermanos
  (woman) i Yermanitha
  (adj) Yermanikos
Germany i Yermania
get (fetch) perno
  have you got...? ehis...?
  to get the train perno to treno
get back: we get back tomorrow
  epistrefoome avrio
  to get something back
  perno kati piso
get in bes mesa
  (arrive) ftano
get out vyeno
get up (rise) sikonome
gift to thoro
gin to 'gin'
girl i kopela
girlfriend i filenatha
give thino
glad efharistimenos
  I'm glad ime eftihis
glass to yali
  (to drink) to potiri
glasses to yalia
gloss prints i yalisteri ektiposi
gloves ta gadia
glue i kola
goggles i maska
gold o hrisos
good kalos
  good! kala!
goodbye ya hara

government i kivernisi
granddaughter i egoni
grandfather o papoos
grandmother i yaya
grandson o egonos
grapes ta stafilia
grass to grasithi
Great Britain i Megali Vretania
Greece i Elatha
Greek *(man)* o Elinas
   (woman) i Elinitha
   (adj) Elinikos
   (language) ta Elinika
Greek orthodox orthothoxos
green prasinos
grey gri
grill i psistaria
grocer *(shop)* to bakaliko
ground floor to isoyio
ground sheet o moosamas
guarantee *(noun)* egi-isi
   (verb) egioome
guard o filakas
guide book o othigos
guitar i kithara
gun *(rifle)* to oplo
   (pistol) to pistoli

hair ta malia
haircut *(for man)* to koorema
   (for woman) to kopsimo
hairdresser i komotria
hair dryer to pistolaki
hair spray i lak
half miso
   half an hour misi ora
half board i demi pansion

ham to zabon
hamburger to hamboorger
hammer to sfiri
hand to heri
handbag i tsada
hand brake to hirofreno
handkerchief to hartomadilo
handle *(door)* to herooli
handsome oreos
hangover o ponokefalos
happy eftihismenos
harbour to limani
hard skliros
   (difficult) thiskolos
hard lenses i skliri faki epafis
hat to kapelo
have eho
   I don't have... then eho...
   can I have...? boro na eho...?
   have you got...? ehete...?
   I have to go now prepi na
   piyeno tora
hayfever o piretos ek hortoo
he aftos
head to kefali
headache o ponokefalos
headlights i provolis
hear akoo-o
hearing aid ta akoostika
heart i karthia
heart attack i karthiaki prosvoli
heating i thermansi
heavy varis
heel i takooni
hello ya soo
help *(noun)* i voithia
   (verb) voitho

help! voiTHia!
her: it's her afti ine
 it's for her ine ya ftin
 give it to her thostis to
 her house to spiti tis
 her shoes ta papootsia tis
 it's hers ine thiko tis
high psilos
highway code o othikos kothikas
hill o lofos
him: it's him aftos ine
 it's for him ine ya fton
 give it to him thostoo to
hire nikiazo
his: his house to spiti too
 his shoes ta papootsia too
 it's his ine thiko too
history i istoria
hitch-hike kano oto-stop
hobby to 'hobby'
Holland i Olanthia
holiday i thiakopes
honest timios
honey to meli
honeymoon o minas too melitos
horn *(car)* to klaxon
 (animal) to kerato
horrible fovero
hospital to nosokomio
hot water bottle i THermofora
hour i ora
house to spiti
how? pos?
hungry: I'm hungry pinao
hurry: I'm in a hurry viazome
husband o sizigos

I ego
ice o pagos
ice cream to pagoto
ice cube to pagaki
ice lolly to pagoto xilaki
if ean
ignition i miza
ill arostos
immediately amesos
impossible athinato
in mesa
India i Inthia
Indian *(man)* o Inthos
 (woman) i Inthi
 (adj) Inthikos
indicator o thiktis
indigestion i thispepsia
infection i molinsi
information i plirofories
injection i enesi
injury to atihima
ink to melani
inner tube i sabrela
insect to edomo
insect repellent o apoTHitis
 edomon
insomnia i aipnia
insurance i asfalia
interesting enthiaferon
interpret thierminevo
invitation i prosklisi
Ireland i Irlanthia
Irish Irlanthikos
Irishman o Irlanthos
Irishwoman i Irlantheza
iron *(metal, for clothes)* to sithero
is: he/she/it is... ine...

island to nisi
it afto
itch *(noun)* i fagoora
  it itches me troi

jacket to sakaki
jacuzzi to 'jacuzzi'
jam i marmelatha
jazz i 'jazz'
jealous ziliaris
jeans to 'jean'
jellyfish i tsoohtra
jeweller to kosmimatopolio
job i thoolia
jog *(verb)* kano 'jogging'
  to go for a jog pao ya
  'jogging'
joke to astio
journey to taxithi
jumper to poolover
just: it's just arrived molis
  eftase
  I've just one left eho mono ena

key to klithi
kidney to nefro
kilo i kilo
kilometre to hiliometro
kitchen i koozina
knee to gonato
knife to maheri
knit pleko
knitting needle i velona pleximatos
know: I don't know then xero

label i etiketa
lace i thantela
laces *(of shoe)* ta korthonia
ladies *(toilet)* i tooaleta yinekon
lake i limni
lamb to arni
lamp i laba
lampshade to labater
land *(noun)* i yi
  (verb) prosyionome
language i glosa
large megalos
last *(final)* telefteos
  last week i perasmeni
  evthomatha
  last month o perasmenos minas
  at last! epi teloos!
late: it's getting late vrathiazi
  the bus is late to leoforio aryise
laugh to yelio
launderette to plidirio roohon
laundry *(place)* to katharistirio
  (dirty clothes) ta aplita
laxative to kathartiko
lazy tebelis
leaf to filo
leaflet to thiafimistiko
learn matheno
leather to therma
left *(not right)* aristera
  there's nothing left
  then emine tipota
left luggage o horos filaxis
  aposkevon
  (locker) to doolapi ton
  aposkevon
leftovers ta apominaria

leg to pothi
lemon to lemoni
lemonade i lemonatha
length to mikos
lens o fakos
less ligotera
lesson to maτhima
letter to grama
letterbox to gramatokivotio
lettuce to marooli
library i vivlioτHiki
licence i athia
life i zoi
lift *(in building)* to asanser
  could you give me a lift?
  borite na me pate?
light *(not heavy)* elafris
  (not dark) apalos
lighter o anaptiras
lighter fuel to aerio anaptira
light meter to fotometro
like: **I like you** moo aresis
  I like swimming moo aresi to
  kolibi
it's like... miazi me...
lime *(fruit)* to kitro
lip salve to vootiro kakao
lipstick to krayion
liqueur to liker
list i lista
litre to litro
litter ta skoopithia
little *(small)* mikros
  it's a little big ine ligo megalo
  just a little ligaki
liver to sikoti
lobster o astakos

lollypop to glifitzoori
long makris
  how long does it take? posi ora
  kani?
lorry to fortigo
lost property i hamenes aposkeves
lot: **a lot** pola
loud thinatos
  (colour) htipitos
lounge to saloni
love *(noun)* i agapi
  (verb) agapo
lover *(man)* o erastis
  (woman) i eromeni
low hamilos
luck i tihi
  good luck! kali tihi!
luggage i aposkeves
luggage rack i skara
lunch to yevma

magazine to periothiko
mail ta gramata
make kano
make-up to 'make-up'
man o adras
manager o thiefτHidis
map o hartis
  a map of Athens enas hartis tis
  AτHinas
marble to marmaro
margarine i margarini
market i agora
marmalade i marmelatha
married padremenos
mascara i maskara
mass *(church)* i litooryia

mast to katarti
match *(light)* to spirto
  (sport) to 'match'
material *(cloth)* to ifasma
mattress to stroma
maybe isos
me: it's me ego ime
  it's for me ine ya mena
  give it to me thosto moo
meal to yevma
meat to kreas
mechanic o mihanikos
medicine to farmako
meeting i sinadisis
melon to peponi
menu to menoo
message to minima
midday to mesimeri
middle: in the middle sti mesi
midnight ta mesanihta
milk to gala
mine: it's mine ine thiko moo
mineral water to emfialomeno
  nero
minute to lepto
mirror o kaтнreftis
mistake to laтнos
  to make a mistake kano laтнos
monastery to monastiri
money ta lefta
month o minas
monument to mnimio
moon to fegari
moped to mihanaki me petalia
more perisoteros
  more or less pano-kato
morning to proi

in the morning to proi
mosaic to psifithoto
mosquito to koonoopi
mother i mitera
motorbike to mihanaki
motorboat i varka me mihani
motorway i eтнniki othos
mountain to voono
mouse to podiki
moustache to moostaki
mouth to stoma
move metakino
  don't move! mi kooniese!
  (house) metakomizo
movie to ergo
Mr. kirios
Mrs. kiria
much: not much ohi poli
mug i koopa
  a mug of coffee ena flitzani
  kafe
mule to moolari
mum i mama
museum to moosio
mushroom to manitari
music i moosiki
musical instrument to moosiko
  organo
musician o moosikos
mussels ta mithia
mustard i moostartha
my: my book to vivlio moo
  my bag i tsada moo
  my keys ta klithia moo
mythology i miтнoloyia

nail *(metal)* to karfi
  (finger) to nihi
nail file i lima nihion
nail polish to mano
name to onoma
nappy i pana
narrow stenos
near: near the door koda sti porta
  near London koda sto Lonthino
necessary aparetitos
necklace to kolie
need *(verb)* hriazome
  I need... hriazome...
  there's no need then hriazete
needle i velona
negative *(photo)* to arnitiko
neither: neither of them kanenas
  apo aftoos
  neither ... nor... oote...
  oote ...
nephew o anipsios
never pote
new kenooryios
news ta nea
newsagent to praktorio
  efimerithon
newspaper i efimeritha
New Zealand i Nea Zilanthia
New Zealander *(man)* o
  Neozilanthos
  (woman) i Neozilantheza
next epomenos
  next week i epomeni
  evthomatha
  next month o epomenos minas
  what next? ti alo?
nice oreos

niece i anipsia
night i nihta
nightclub to nihterino kedro
nightdress to nihtiko
no *(response)* ohi
  I have no money then eho lefta
noisy THorivothis
north o voras
Northern Ireland i Vorios Irlanthia
nose i miti
not then
notebook to blokaki
nothing tipota
novel to miTHistorima
now tora
nowhere pooTHena
nudist o yimnistis
number o ariTHmos
number plate i pinakitha
nurse i nosokoma
nut *(fruit)* i xiri karpi
  (for bolt) to paximathi

occasionally pote-pote
octopus to htapothi
of too
office to grafio
often sihna
oil to lathi
ointment i alifi
OK edaxi
old palios
olive i elia
omelette i omeleta
on pano
one enas, mia, ena

onion to kremithi
only mono
open *(verb)* anigo
　　(adj) anihtos
opposite: opposite the hotel
　　apenadi apo to xenothohio
optician o optikos
or i
orange *(colour)* portokali
　　(fruit) to portokali
orange juice i portokalatha
orchestra i orhistra
ordinary *(normal)* kanonikos
organ to organo
　　(music) to armonio
our: our house to spiti mas
　　it's ours ine thiko mas
out: he's out ine exo
outside exo
over pano apo
　　over there eki pera
overtake posperno
oyster to strithi

package to paketo
　　(parcel) to thema
packet to paketo
　　a packet of... ena paketo...
pack of cards i trapoola
padlock to looketo
page i selitha
pain o ponos
paint *(noun)* to hroma
pair to zevgari
Pakistan to Pakistan
Pakistani *(man)* o Pakistanos
　　(woman) i Pakistani

(adj) Pakistanikos
pale hlomos
pancakes i thiples
paper to harti
paracetamol to pafsipono
parcel to thema
pardon? signomi?
parents o gonis
park *(noun)* to parko
　　(verb) parkaro
parsley o maidanos
party *(celebration)* to parti
　　(group) to groop
　　(political) to koma
passenger epivatis
passport to thiavatirio
pasta ta zimarika
path to monopati
pavement to pezothromio
pay plirono
peach to rothakino
peanuts ta fistikia
pear to ahlathi
pearl to margaritari
peas ta bizelia
pedestrian o pezos
peg *(clothes)* i kremastra
pen to stilo
pencil to molivi
pencil sharpener i xistra
penfriend o filos thi'alilografias
peninsula i hersonisos
penknife o sooyas
people i anthropi
pepper *(& salt)* to piperi
　　(red/green) i piperia
peppermints i medes

per: per night tin vrathia

perfect telios

perfume to aroma

perhaps isos

perm i permanant

petrol i venzini

petrol station to venzinathiko

petticoat to kobinezon

photograph (noun) i fotografia
   (verb) fotografizo

photographer o fotografos

phrase book to vivlio xenon
   thialogon

piano to piano

pickpocket o portofolas

picnic to 'picnic'

pillow to maxilari

pilot o pilotos

pin i karfitsa

pine (tree) to pefko

pineapple o ananas

pink roz

pipe (for smoking) to tsibooki
   (for water) i solina

piston to pistoni

pizza i pizza

place to meros

plant to fito

plaster (for cut) o lefkoplastis

plastic to plastiko

plastic bag i plastiki sakoola

plate to piato

platform i platforma

play (theatre) to THeatriko
   ergo

please parakalo

plug (electrical) i briza

(sink) i tsepi

poison to thilitirio

police i astinomia

police station to astinomiko
   tmima

policeman o astinomikos

politics ta politika

poor ftohos
   (bad quality) kakos

pop music i pop moosiki

pork to hirino

port (harbour) to limani

porter (for luggage) o ah-THoforos
   (hotel) o THiroros

possible thinaton

post (noun) ta gramata
   (verb) tahithromo

post box to gramatokivotio

postcard i kart-postal

poster to poster

postman o tahithromos

post office to tahithromio

potato i patata

poultry ta poolerika

pound (money) i lira
   (weight) i libra

powder i skoni

pram to karotsaki

prawn i garitha
   (bigger) i karavitha

prescription i sidayi

pretty (beautiful) omorfos
   (quite) arketos

priest o papas

private ithiotikos

problem to provlima
   what's the problem? ti simveni?

120

public to kino
pull travo
puncture to kedima
purple mov
purse to portofoli
push sprohno
pushchair to karotsaki
pyjamas i pitzames

quality i piotita
quay i prokimea
question i erotisi
queue *(noun)* i oora
  (verb) beno stin oora
quick grigoros
quiet isihos
quite *(fairly)* arketa
  (fully) telios

radiator to psiyio
radio to rathiofono
radish to rapanaki
railway line i grames too trenoo
rain i vrohi
raincoat to athiavroho
raisins i stafithes
rare *(uncommon)* spanios
  (steak) misopsimenos
rat o arooreos
razor blades ta xirafakia
read thiavazo
reading lamp to fos too grafioo
  (bed) to potatif
ready etimos
rear lights ta piso fota
receipt i apothixi
receptionist o resepsionistas

record *(music)* o thiskos
  (sporting etc) to rekor
record player to pik-ap
record shop to thiskopolio
red kokino
refreshments ta anapsiktika
registered letter to sistimeno
  grama
relative o sigenis
relax iremo
religion i THriskia
remember THimame
  I don't remember then
  THimame
rent *(verb)* nikiazo
reservation to klisimo THesis
rest *(remainder)* to ipolipo
  (relax) xekoorazome
restaurant to estiatorio
return epistrefo
Rhodes i Rothos
rice to rizi
rich ploosios
right *(correct)* sostos
  (direction) thexia
ring *(to call)* tilefono
  (wedding etc) to thahtilithi
ripe orimos
river to potami
road o thromos
rock *(stone)* o vrahos
  (music) i moosiki rok
roll *(bread)* to psomaki
  (verb) kilo
roller skates ta patinia
roof i orofi
  (flat) i taratsa

room to thomatio
  (space) to meros
rope to s-hini
rose to triadafilo
round *(circular)* strogilos
  it's my round ine i sira moo
rowing boat i varka me koopia
rubber *(eraser)* i goma
  (material) to lastiho
rubbish ta skoopithia
ruby *(stone)* to roobini
rucksack to sakithio
rug *(mat)* to halaki
  (blanket) i kooverta
ruins ta eripia
ruler o harakas
rum to roomi
run *(person)* treho
runway o thiathromos

sad lipimenos
safe asfalis
safety pin i paramana
sailing boat to istioforo
salad i salata
salami to salami
sale *(at reduced prices)* i ekptosis
salmon o solomos
salt to alati
same: the same dress to ithio
  forema
  the same people i ithi-i anthropi
  the same again please ena
  akoma
sand i amos
sandals ta sadalia
sand dunes i amolofi

sandwich to 'sandwich'
sanitary towels i servietes
sauce i saltsa
saucepan i katsarola
sauna i sona
sausage to lookaniko
say lego
  what did you say? ti ipes?
  how do you say...? pos тна
  poome...?
scarf to kaskol
  (head) to madili
school to s-holio
scissors ta psalithi
Scottish Skotsezikos
Scotland i Skotia
screw i vitha
screwdriver to katsavithi
sea i тнalasa
seafood ta тнalasina
seat i тнesi
seat belt i zoni asfalias
second thefteros
see kitazo
  I can't see then vlepo
  I see katalava
sell poolo
sellotape® to 'sellotape'
separate xehoristos
separated horismenos
serious sovaros
serviette i hartopetseta
several arketi
sew ravo
shampoo to sambooan
shave *(noun)* to xirisma
  (verb) xirizome

shaving foam o afros xirismatos

shawl to sali

she afti

sheet to sedoni

shell to ostrako

sherry to seri

ship to karavi

shirt to pookamiso

shoe laces ta korthonia

shoe polish to verniki papootsion

shoe shop to katastima ipothimaton

shoes ta papootsia

shop to magazi

shopping ta psonia
  to go shopping pao ya psonia

short kodos

shorts to 'shorts'

shoulder o omos

shower *(bath)* to doos
  (rain) i bora

shrimp i garitha

shutter *(camera)* to thiafragma
  (window) to exofilo

sick *(ill)* arostos
  I feel sick ime athiatHetos

side *(edge)* plevra
  I'm on her side ime me to meros tis

sidelights ta fota porias

sights: the sights of... ta axiotHeata tis...

silk to metaxoto

silver *(colour)* asimi
  (metal) to asimi

simple aplos

sing tragootho

single *(one)* monos
  (unmarried) anipadros

single room to mono thomatio

sister i athelfi

skid *(verb)* glistrao

skin cleanser to galaktoma kaтHarismoo

skirt i foosta

sky o ooranos

sleep *(noun)* o ipnos
  (verb) kimame
  to go to sleep pao ya ipno

sleeping bag to 'sleeping bag'

sleeping pill to ipnotiko hapi

slippers i padofles

slow argos

small mikros

smell *(noun)* i mirothia
  (verb) mirizo

smile *(noun)* to hamoyelo
  (verb) hamoyelo

smoke *(noun)* o kapnos
  (verb) kapnizo

snack to prohiro yevma

snorkel o anapnefstiras

snow to hioni

so: so good poli kala
  not so much ohi toso poli

soaking solution *(for contact lenses)* igro sidirisis fakon epafis

socks i kaltses

soda water i sotha

soft lenses i malaki faki epafis

somebody kapios

somehow kapos

something kati

sometimes merikes fores
somewhere kapoo
son o yios
song to tragoothi
sorry! pardon!
   I'm sorry signomi
soup i soopa
south o notos
South Africa i Notios Afriki
South African (man) o
   Notioafrikanos
   (woman) i Notioafrikana
   (adj) Notioafrikanikos
souvenir to enтHimio
spade (shovel) to ftiari
   (cards) to bastooni
Spain i Ispania
Spanish (adj) Ispanikos
spanner to klithi
spares ta adalaktika
spark(ing) plug to boozi
speak milao
   do you speak...? milate...?
   I don't speak... then milo...
speed i tahitita
speed limit to orio tahititos
speedometer to konter
spider i arahni
spinach to spanaki
spoon to kootali
sprain to strabooligma
spring (mechanical) to elatirio
   (season) i anixi
stadium to stathio
staircase i skala
stairs ta skalopatia
stamp to gramatosimo

stapler o sinthetiras
star to asteri
   (film) i star
start i arhi
   (verb) arhizo
station to staтHmos
statue to agalma
steak i brizola
steal klevo
   it's been stolen to klepsane
steering wheel to timoni
stewardess i aerosinothos
sting (noun) to tsooximo
   (verb) tsoozo
   it stings tsoozi
stockings i kaltses
stomach to stomahi
stomach ache o stomahoponos
stop (verb) stamato
   (bus stop) i stasi
   stop! stamata!
storm i тHiela
strawberry i fraoola
stream (small river) to potamaki
street o thromos
string (cord) o spagos
   (guitar etc) i horthi
student o maтHitis
stupid vlakas
suburbs ta proastia
sugar i zahari
suit (noun) to koostoomi
   (verb) teriazo
   it suits you soo pai
suitcase i valitsa
sun o ilios
sunbathe kano ilioтHerapia

sunburn to kapsimo apo ton ilio
sunglasses ta yalia ilioo
sunny: it's sunny ehi liakatha
suntan to mavrisma
suntan lotion to adiliako
supermarket to 'supermarket'
supplement epipleon
surname to epiTHeto
sweat *(noun)* o ithrotas
   (verb) ithrono
sweatshirt i fanela
sweet *(not sour)* glikos
   (candy) i karamela
swimming costume to mayio
swimming pool i pisina
swimming trunks to mayio
switch o thiakoptis
synagogue i sinagoyi

table to trapezi
tablet to thiskio
take perno
take away ya to thromo
take off *(noun)* i apoyiosi
   (verb) apoyionome
talcum powder to talk
talk *(noun)* i sizitisi
   (verb) milo
tall psilos
tampon to tampax®
tangerine to mandarini
tap i vrisi
tapestry i tapetsaria
tea to tsai
tea towel i petseta
telegram to tilegrafima
telephone *(noun)* to tilefono

   (verb) tilefono
telephone box o tilefonikos
   THalamos
telephone call to tilefonima
television i tileorasi
temperature i THermokrasia
tent i skini
tent peg o pasalos skinis
tent pole o stilos skinis
thank *(verb)* efharisto
   thanks efharisto
   thank you sas efharisto
that: that bus ekino to leoforio
   that man ekinos o adras
   that woman ekini i yineka
   what's that? ti ine ekino?
   I think that... nomizo oti...
their: their room to thomatio toos
   their books ta vivlia toos
   it's theirs ine thiko toos
them: it's them afti ine
   it's for them ine yaftoos
   give it to them thosto toos
then tote
there eki
thermos flask o THermos
these: these things afta ta
   pragmata
   these are mine afta ine thika
   moo
they afti
thick pahis
thin leptos
think nomizo
   I think so etsi nomizo
   I'll think about it THa to
   skefto

thirsty: **I'm thirsty** thipso
this: **this bus** afto to leoforio
  this man aftos o adras
  this woman afti i yineka
  what's this? ti ine afto?
  this is Mr... apotho o kirios...
those: **those things** afta ta
  pragmata
  those are his afta ine thika too
throat o lemos
throat pastilles i pastilies lemoo
thunderstorm i kateyitha
ticket to isitirio
tie *(noun)* i gravata
  (verb) theno
time i ora
  what's the time? ti ora ine?
timetable to programa
tin i konserva
tin opener to anihtiri
tip *(money)* to poorbooar
  (end) i miti
tired koorasmenos
  I feel tired ime koorasmenos
tissues ta hartomadila
to: **to England** stin Aglia
  to the station sto staTHmo
  to the doctor sto yatro
toast to tost
tobacco o kapnos
toilet i tooaleta
toilet paper to harti iyias
tomato i domata
tomorrow avrio
tongue i glosa
tonic to 'tonic'
tonight apopse

too *(also)* episis
  (excessive) para poli
toothache o ponothodos
toothbrush i othodovoortsa
toothpaste i othodokrema
torch o fakos
tour i peri-iyisi
tourist o tooristas
towel i petseta
tower o pirgos
town i poli
town hall to thimarhio
toy to pehnithi
toy shop to katastima pehnithion
track suit i aTHlitiki forma
tractor to trakter
tradition i parathosi
traffic i kinisi
traffic lights ta fanaria
trailer to rimoolko
train to treno
translate metafrazo
transmission *(for car)* i metathosi
  kiniseos
travel agency to taxithiotiko
  grafio
traveller's cheque i taxithiotiki
  epitayi
tray o thiskos
tree to thedro
trousers to padeloni
try prospaTHo
tunnel i siraga
Turk *(man)* o Toorkos
  (woman) i Toorkala
Turkey i Toorkia
Turkish Toorkikos

tweezers to tsibithaki
typewriter i grafomihani
tyre to lastiho

umbrella i obrela
uncle o THios
under kato
underground o ipoyios
underpants to sovrako
university to panepistimio
unmarried anipadros
until mehri
unusual asiniTHistos
up pano
 (upwards) pros ta pano
urgent epigon
us: it's us emis imaste
 it's for us ine ya mas
 give it to us thosto mas
use *(noun)* i hrisimotis
 (verb) hrisimopio
 it's no use then axizi ton kopo
useful hrisimos
usual siniTHismenos
usually siniTHos

vacancy *(room)* kenos
vacuum cleaner i ilektriki skoopa
vacuum flask o THermos
valley i kilatha
valve i valvitha
vanilla i vanilia
vase to vazo
veal to mos-haraki
vegetables ta lahanika
vegetarian *(person)* o hortofagos
vehicle to trohoforo

very poli
vest to fanelaki
view i THea
viewfinder to skopeftro
villa i 'villa'
village to horio
vinegar to xithi
violin to violi
visa i viza
visit *(noun)* i episkepsi
 (verb) episkeptome
visitor o episkeptis
vitamin tablet i vitamini
vodka i vodka
voice i foni

waiter o servitoros
 waiter! garson!
waiting room to saloni
waitress i garsona
Wales i Ooalia
walk *(noun)* to perpatima
 (verb) perpato
 to go for a walk pao volta
walkman® to 'walkman'®
wall o tihos
wallet to portofoli
war o polemos
wardrobe i doolapa
warm zestos
was: I was imoon
 he/she/it was itan
washing powder to aporipadiko
washing-up liquid to igro
 piaton
wasp i sfiga
watch *(noun)* to roloi

(verb) parakolooᴛʜo
water to nero
waterfall o katarahtis
wave *(noun)* to kima
  (verb) hereto
we emis
weather o keros
wedding o gamos
week i evthomatha
wellingtons i galotses
Welsh Ooalikos
were: we were imastan
  you were isastan
  (sing. familiar) isoon
  they were itan
west thitikos
wet vregmenos
what? ti?
wheel i rotha
wheelchair i anapiriki polithrona
when? pote?
where? poote?
whether kata poso
which? pios?
whisky to 'whisky'
white aspros
who? pios?
why? yati?
wide platis
wife i sizigos
wind o anemos
window to paraᴛʜiro
windscreen to parbriz
windscreen wiper o
  ialokaᴛʜaristiras
wine to krasi
wine list o katalogos krasion

wing to ftero
with me
without horis
wood to xilo
wool to mali
word i lexi
work *(noun)* i thoolia
  (verb) thoolevo
worry beads to kobolo-i
wrapping paper harti peritiligmatos
  (for presents) harti ya thora
wrist o karpos
writing paper to harti alilografias
wrong laᴛʜos

year o hronos
yellow kitrinos
yes ne
yesterday htes
yet akoma
  not yet ohi akoma
yoghurt to yaoorti
you esis *(sing. familiar)* esi
your: your book *(familiar)* to
  vivlio soo
  (polite) to vivlio sas
  your shoes *(familiar)* ta
  papootsia soo
  (polite) ta papootsia sas
yours: is it yours? *(familiar)* ine
  thiko soo?
  (polite) ine thiko sas?
youth hostel o xenonas neon
Yugoslavia i Yoogoslavia
Yugoslavian Yoogoslavikos
zip to fermooar
zoo zo-oloyikos kipos